145 Juice, Salad, and Meal Recipes to Fight Cancer

The Comprehensive Guide to Fighting Cancer

By

Joe Correa CSN

COPYRIGHT

© 2019 Live Stronger Faster Inc.

All rights reserved

Reproduction or translation of any part of this work beyond that permitted by section 107 or 108 of the 1976 United States Copyright Act without the permission of the copyright owner is unlawful.

This publication is designed to provide accurate and authoritative information in regard to the subject matter covered. It is sold with the understanding that neither the author nor the publisher is engaged in rendering medical advice. If medical advice or assistance is needed, consult with a doctor. This book is considered a guide and should not be used in any way detrimental to your health. Consult with a physician before starting this nutritional plan to make sure it's right for you.

ACKNOWLEDGEMENTS

This book is dedicated to my friends and family that have had mild or serious illnesses so that you may find a solution and make the necessary changes in your life.

145 Juice, Salad, and Meal Recipes to Fight Cancer

The Comprehensive Guide to Fighting Cancer

By

Joe Correa CSN

CONTENTS

Copyright

Acknowledgements

About The Author

Introduction

Commitment

145 Juice, Salad, and Meal Recipes to Fight Cancer: The Comprehensive Guide to Fighting Cancer

Additional Titles from This Author

ABOUT THE AUTHOR

After years of Research, I honestly believe in the positive effects that proper nutrition can have over the body and mind. My knowledge and experience has helped me live healthier throughout the years and which I have shared with family and friends. The more you know about eating and drinking healthier, the sooner you will want to change your life and eating habits.

Nutrition is a key part in the process of being healthy and living longer so get started today. The first step is the most important and the most significant.

INTRODUCTION

145 Juice, Salad, and Meal Recipes to Fight Cancer: The Comprehensive Guide to Fighting Cancer

By Joe Correa CSN

Having in mind that cancer is the second-leading cause of death in the world, it is very important to recognize early symptoms which, when treated on time, can save your life. These symptoms often include fatigue, changes in bowel or bladder habits, weight changes, lumps that can be felt under the skin, trouble breathing, persistent cough, skin changes, unexplained bleeding or bruising, unexplained fevers, etc. If you have any persistent symptoms that concern you, it is crucial to make an appointment with your doctor.

One of the major causes for this disease is our modern lifestyles which surround us with different toxins, cancerous substances, and stress. But the main reason is probably poor nutrition for most people. The lack of basic nutrients weakens our immune system which leads to serious and long-term damage to your health and eventually becomes cancer. Most food is full of artificial flavors, colors, additives, stabilizers, and preservatives. Although some of these substances are harmless, many of them are extremely toxic and can deprive our organism of some important nutrients. Although most people know these facts, in theory, they can't seem to find enough time to plan their meals on a daily basis, which is why fast food has become so popular.

-These cancer preventing recipes are designed to give you exactly that, all the important nutrients in just a couple of minutes. Start today and see the changes in your life!

COMMITMENT

In order to improve my condition, I *(your name)*, commit to eating more of these foods on a daily basis and to exercise at least 30 minutes daily:

- Berries (especially blueberries), peaches, cherries, apples, apricots, oranges, lemon juice, grapefruit, tangerines, mandarins, pears, etc.
- Broccoli, spinach, collard greens, sweet potatoes, avocado, artichoke, baby corn, carrots, celery, cauliflower, onions, etc.
- Whole grains, steel-cut oats, oatmeal, quinoa, barley, etc.
- Black beans, red bean beans, garbanzo beans, lentils, etc.
- Nuts and seeds including: walnuts, cashews, flaxseeds, sesame seeds, etc.
- Fish
- 8 – 10 glasses of water

Sign here

X_____

145 JUICE, SALAD, AND MEAL RECIPES TO FIGHT CANCER: THE COMPREHENSIVE GUIDE TO FIGHTING CANCER

JUICE RECIPES

1. Sweet Potato Carrot Juice

Ingredients:

2 large carrots

1 small sweet potato, peeled

2 medium-sized green apples, cored

1 large orange, peeled

¼ tsp of pumpkin pie spice

Preparation:

Combine all ingredients except pumpkin pie spice in a juicer and process until juiced. Transfer the juice to serving glasses and add few ice cubes. Sprinkle with some pumpkin pie spice and serve.

Nutritional information per serving: Kcal: 147, Protein: 2.1g, Carbs: 35.4g, Fats: 0.1g

2. Ginger Chia Juice

Ingredients:

3 large carrots

2 large apples, cored

½ tsp of ginger, ground

1 tbsp of chia seeds

Preparation:

Combine all ingredients except chia seeds in a juicer and process until juiced.

Transfer to serving glasses and add few ice cubes. Sprinkle with chia seeds before serving for extra nutrients. Enjoy!

Nutritional information per serving: Kcal: 177, Protein: 3.2g, Carbs: 28.4g, Fats: 4.6g

3. Kale Squash Juice

Ingredients:

¼ cup of fresh kale

½ yellow squash, peeled

1 medium-sized broccoli

1 large apple, cored

¼ cup of fresh spinach

4 small carrots

Preparation:

Combine all ingredients in a juicer and process until juiced.

Transfer to serving glasses and add few ice cubes. Serve immediately.

Nutritional information per serving: Kcal: 81, Protein: 2.3g, Carbs: 18.4g, Fats: 0.2g

4. Watermelon Juice

Ingredients:

1 cup of watermelon, peeled and seeded

1 cup of pineapple, peeled

½ large lemon, peeled

½ tsp of ginger, ground

Preparation:

Combine all ingredients in a juicer and process until juiced.

Transfer to serving glasses and add few ice cubes. Serve immediately!

Nutritional information per serving: Kcal: 41, Protein: 1.4g, Carbs: 10.2g, Fats: 0.1g

5. Cancun Juice

Ingredients:

½ cup of fresh kale

1 large lime, peeled

1 large cucumber

1 celery stalk

1 small jalapeno pepper, seeded

Preparation:

Combine all ingredients in a juicer and process until juiced. Add coconut water if it is too spicy.

Transfer to serving glasses and add a few ice cubes.

Serve immediately.

Nutritional information per serving: Kcal: 171, Protein: 3.2g, Carbs: 47.3g, Fats: 1.3g

6. Flaxseed Brown Juice

Ingredients:

2 large carrots

½ cup of fresh spinach

2 tbsp of fresh parsley

2 large apples, cored

¼ tsp of ginger, ground

1 tbsp of flaxseeds

Preparation:

Combine all ingredients in a juicer except flaxseeds. Process until juiced.

Transfer to serving glasses and add few ice cubes.

Sprinkle with flaxseeds and serve!

Nutritional information per serving: Kcal: 119, Protein: 4.3g, Carbs: 62.2g, Fats: 2.3g

7. Lemon Kale Juice

Ingredients:

½ cup of fresh kale

1 lemon, peeled

2 large green apples, cored

1 large pear, cored

Preparation:

Combine all ingredients in a juicer and process until juiced.

Transfer to serving glasses and add few ice cubes before serving.

Enjoy!

Nutritional information per serving: Kcal: 120, Protein: 3.2g, Carbs: 62.5g, Fats: 1.2g

8. Broccoli Juice

Ingredients:

1 cup of broccoli

2 large oranges, peeled

1 large cucumber, peeled

1 large carrot

Preparation:

Combine all ingredients in a juicer and process until juiced.

Transfer to serving glasses and add few ice cubes.

Serve immediately!

Nutritional information per serving: Kcal: 68, Protein: 2.3g, Carbs: 19.7g, Fats: 0.1g

9. Collard Green Juice

Ingredients:

½ cup of collard greens

½ tsp of ginger, ground

1 large cucumber

¼ cup of fresh parsley

1 large apple, cored

Preparation:

Combine all ingredients in a juicer and process until juiced.

Transfer to serving glasses and add few ice cubes.

Serve immediately.

Nutritional information per serving: Kcal: 96, Protein: 3.1g, Carbs: 28.7g, Fats: 1.2g

10. Fennel Tangerine Juice

Ingredients:

1 large fennel

½ cup of fresh kale

1 large green apple, cored

4 tangerines, peeled

Preparation:

Place all ingredients in a juicer and process until juiced.

Transfer to serving glasses and add few ice cubes or refrigerate before use.

Nutritional information per serving: Kcal: 121, Protein: 4.3g, Carbs: 31.3g, Fats: 1.3g

11. Green Grape Juice

Ingredients:

1 cup of green grapes

2 large cucumbers

1 large pear, cored

1 lime, peeled

Preparation:

Combine all ingredients in a juicer and process until juiced.

Transfer to serving glasses and refrigerate for 30 minutes before serving.

Nutritional information per serving: Kcal: 113, Protein: 18.3g, Carbs: 31.3g, Fats: 0.1g

12. Watercress Juice

Ingredients:

½ cup of watercress

2 large green apples, cored

1 large lemon, peeled

1 large lime, peeled

Preparation:

Combine all ingredients except chia seeds in a juicer and process until juiced.

Transfer to serving glasses and add few ice cubes.

Serve immediately.

Nutritional information per serving: Kcal: 101, Protein: 17.2g, Carbs: 28.8g, Fats: 0.2g

13. Pineapple Cantaloupe Juice

Ingredients:

1 cup of cantaloupe, peeled

½ pineapple, peeled

2 large green apples, cored

½ cup of fresh kale

Preparation:

Combine all ingredients in a juicer and process until juiced.

Transfer to serving glasses and add few ice cubes, or refrigerate for 30 minutes before serving.

Nutritional information per serving: Kcal: 115, Protein: 1.2g, Carbs: 28.8g, Fats: 1.2g

14. Radish Fennel Juice

Ingredients:

6 medium-sized radishes

1 small fennel

1 large orange, peeled

5 large celery stalks

1 large cucumber

Preparation:

Combine all ingredients in a juicer and process until juiced.

Transfer to serving glasses and refrigerate for a while before serving.

Nutritional information per serving: Kcal: 110, Protein: 6.1g, Carbs: 28.7g, Fats: 1.2g

15. Swiss Chard Basil Juice

Ingredients:

½ cup of Swiss chard

½ cup of fresh basil

1 large lime, peeled

2 large green apples, cored

¼ cup of fresh mint

Preparation:

Combine all ingredients in a juicer and process until juiced.

Transfer to serving glasses and add few ice cubes or refrigerate until use.

Nutritional information per serving: Kcal: 114, Protein: 2.3g, Carbs: 30.4g, Fats: 0.2g

16. Green Cabbage Juice

Ingredients:

½ cup of green cabbage

4 celery stalks

1 large green apple, cored

3 large carrots

1 large lemon, peeled

1 tbsp of liquid honey

Preparation:

Combine all ingredients in a juicer and process until juiced.

Transfer to serving glasses and refrigerate for 20 minutes before serving.

Nutritional information per serving: Kcal: 162, Protein: 3.1g, Carbs: 39.3g, Fats: 0.1g

17. Grapefruit Rosemary Juice

Ingredients:

3 large grapefruits, peeled

3 large oranges, peeled

1 large lemon, peeled

½ tsp of fresh rosemary

Preparation:

Combine all ingredients in a juicer and process until juiced.

Transfer to serving glasses and add few ice cubes.

Sprinkle with fresh rosemary and serve immediately!

Nutritional information per serving: Kcal: 140, Protein: 3.4g, Carbs: 37.6g, Fats: 0.1g

18. Strawberry Peach Juice

Ingredients:

3 large peaches, pitted

1 cup of strawberries

1 large green apple, cored

¼ tsp of ginger, ground

Preparation:

Combine all ingredients in a juicer and process until juiced.

Transfer to serving glasses and add few ice cubes, or refrigerate for 1 hour before serving.

Nutritional information per serving: Kcal: 64, Protein: 1.2g, Carbs: 18.3g, Fats: 0.1g

19. Cilantro Juice

Ingredients:

½ cup of cilantro

3 celery stalks

1 large green apple, cored

1 large lemon, peeled

½ tsp of ginger, ground

Preparation:

Combine all ingredients except ginger in a juicer.

Process until juiced and transfer to serving glasses and stir in the ginger.

Add few ice cubes and serve immediately.

Nutritional information per serving: Kcal: 73, Protein: 2.2g, Carbs: 26.7g, Fats: 0.1g

20. Pomegranate Kale Juice

Ingredients:

½ cup of pomegranate seeds

½ cup of fresh kale

1 large green apple, cored

¼ tsp of ginger, ground

3-4 fresh mint leaves

Preparation:

Combine pomegranate seeds, kale, mint, and apple in a juicer and process until juiced.

Transfer to serving glasses and stir in the ginger and some extra pomegranate seeds if you like.

Add few ice cubes and serve immediately.

Nutritional information per serving: Kcal: 143, Protein: 6.2g, Carbs: 41.2g, Fats: 2.4g

21. Tomato Garlic Juice

Ingredients:

2 large tomatoes, halved

2 garlic cloves, peeled

3 large cucumbers

1 large bell pepper, seeded

1 small shallot

1 large lime, peeled

¼ cup of fresh cilantro

Preparation:

Combine all ingredients in a juicer and process until juiced.

Transfer to serving glasses and add few ice cubes or refrigerate for a while before serving.

Nutritional information per serving: Kcal: 109, Protein: 6.4g, Carbs: 38.5g, Fats: 1.2g

22. Pineapple Carrot Juice

Ingredients:

1 cup of pineapple, peeled

2 large carrots

½ cup of watercress

1 large lemon, peeled

¼ tsp of ginger root

Preparation:

Combine all ingredients in a juicer and process until juiced.

Transfer to serving glasses and enjoy!

Nutritional information per serving: Kcal: 101, Protein: 3.1g, Carbs: 34.2g, Fats: 1.1g

23. Strawberry Kiwi Juice

Ingredients:

2 kiwis, peeled

1 large cucumber

1 cup of fresh strawberries

1 small lime, peeled

2 tbsp of fresh mint

Preparation:

Combine all ingredients in a juicer and process until juiced.

Transfer to serving glasses and refrigerate for a while until use.

Nutritional information per serving: Kcal: 91, Protein: 3.1g, Carbs: 29.9g, Fats: 0.9g

24. Apple Chia Juice

Ingredients:

1 large red apple, cored

1 large lemon, peeled

1 large bell pepper, seeded

3 tbsp of chia seeds

Preparation:

Combine apple, lemon, and bell pepper and run trough juicer.

Process until juiced and stir in the chia seeds.

Let it stand for 15 minutes to thicken and stir well before use.

Nutritional information per serving: Kcal: 135, Protein: 4.2g, Carbs: 31.3g, Fats: 6.2g

25. Spicy Grapefruit Juice

Ingredients:

1 large kiwi, peeled

½ medium-sized grapefruit, peeled

1 large lemon, peeled

3 celery stalks

¼ tsp of ginger, ground

¼ tsp of Cayenne pepper, ground

A handful of watercress

Preparation:

Combine kiwi, grapefruit, lemon, celery, and watercress in a juicer and process until juiced.

Transfer to serving glasses and stir in the ginger and cayenne pepper.

Enjoy!

Nutritional information per serving: Kcal: 61, Protein: 2.1g, Carbs: 20.4g, Fats: 1.1g

26. Turmeric Cucumber Juice

Ingredients:

1 large cucumber

1 cup of pineapple, chopped

3 celery stalks

½ cup of fresh spinach

¼ tsp of ginger, ground

¼ tsp of turmeric, ground

Preparation:

Combine all ingredients except ginger and turmeric in a juicer.

Process until juiced and transfer to serving glasses. Stir in the turmeric and ginger and serve.

Nutritional information per serving: Kcal: 109, Protein: 3.3g, Carbs: 61.2g, Fats: 1.3g

27. Zucchini Roma Juice

Ingredients:

2 medium-sized zucchini

1 garlic clove, peeled

6 asparagus stalks

3 Roma tomatoes

4 large carrots

Preparation:

Combine all ingredients in a juicer and process until juiced.

Transfer to serving glasses and enjoy immediately.

Nutritional information per serving: Kcal: 92, Protein: 5.4g, Carbs: 27.3g, Fats: 0.9g

28. Cinnamon Chia Juice

Ingredients:

1 tbsp of chia seeds

1 large apple, cored

1 cup of fresh spinach

¼ tsp of cinnamon, ground

Preparation:

Combine apple and spinach in a juicer and process until juiced.

Transfer to serving glasses and stir in the cinnamon and chia seeds.

Set aside for 20 minutes to thicken, then serve.

Nutritional information per serving: Kcal: 121, Protein: 4.3g, Carbs: 27.8g, Fats: 5.3g

29. Green Coconut Juice

Ingredients:

1 large lime, peeled

3 oz of coconut water

5 small celery stalks

¼ cup od fresh mint

¼ cup of fresh spinach

Preparation:

Combine lime, celery, spinach, and mint in a juicer and process until juiced.

Transfer to serving glasses and stir in coconut water. Refrigerate for 20 minutes before use.

Nutritional information per serving: Kcal: 45, Protein: 2.2g, Carbs: 16.8g, Fats: 1.6g

30. Cauliflower Broccoli Juice

Ingredients:

2 cups of cauliflower, chopped

1 cup of fresh broccoli

4 large carrots

1 large green apple, cored

1 tsp of ginger root

Preparation:

Combine all ingredients in a juicer and process until juiced.

Transfer to serving glasses and garnish with mint or add ice cubes for refreshment.

Enjoy!

Nutritional information per serving: Kcal: 136, Protein: 6.3g, Carbs: 42.8g, Fats: 1.2g

31. Ice Green Juice

Ingredients:

1 medium-sized cucumber

1 large pear, cored

3 large carrots

1 large lemon, peeled

¼ cup of fresh mint

½ cup of broccoli

1 tsp of ginger root

½ tsp of green tea powder

2 oz of water

Preparation:

Combine cucumber, pear, carrots, lemon, mint, ginger, and broccoli in a juicer and process until juiced.

Mix water with green tea in a serving glasses and add juice.

Mix with a spoon and add few ice cubes. Serve immediately.

Nutritional information per serving: Kcal: 141, Protein: 5.5g, Carbs: 45.7g, Fats: 0.9g

32. Orange Green Juice

Ingredients:

2 large oranges, peeled

½ cup of fresh broccoli, chopped

3 large carrots

4 collard green leaves

4 fresh kale leaves

1 garlic clove, peeled

Preparation:

Combine all ingredients in a juicer and process until juiced.

Transfer to serving glasses and serve immediately.

Nutritional information per serving: Kcal: 171, Protein: 9.2g, Carbs: 43.3g, Fats: 2.3g

33. Orange Honey Juice

Ingredients:

2 large oranges, peeled

½ cup of grapefruit, chopped

3-4 fresh kale leaves

1 tsp of liquid honey

¼ tsp of ginger, ground

Preparation:

Combine oranges, grapefruit, and kale in a juicer and process until juiced.

Transfer to serving glasses and stir in the honey and ginger.

Serve immediately.

Nutritional information per serving: Kcal: 128, Protein: 7.3g, Carbs: 34.5g, Fats: 1.1g

34. Sweet Potato Ginger Juice

Ingredients:

2 medium-sized sweet potatoes, peeled

1 large peach, pitted and halved

¼ tsp of ginger, ground

¼ tsp of cinnamon, ground

Preparation:

Combine potatoes and peach in a juicer and process until juiced.

Transfer to serving glasses and stir in the ginger and cinnamon.

Serve immediately.

Nutritional information per serving: Kcal: 159, Protein: 5.2g, Carbs: 50.1g, Fats: 0.9g

35. Strawberry Tomato Juice

Ingredients:

1 cup of fresh strawberries

2 large tomatoes

2 large carrots

1 large orange, peeled

1 large bell pepper, seeded

Preparation:

Combine all ingredients in a juicer and process until juiced.

Transfer to serving glasses and refrigerate for 30 minutes before serving.

Nutritional information per serving: Kcal: 104, Protein: 3.9g, Carbs: 31.2g, Fats: 1.1g

36. Orange Turmeric Juice

Ingredients:

1 large orange bell pepper, seeded

1 large orange, peeled

1 large carrot

1 large lemon, peeled

1 small cucumber

¼ tsp of turmeric, ground

Preparation:

Combine all ingredients except turmeric in a juicer and process until juiced.

Transfer to serving glasses and stir in the turmeric. Serve immediately.

Nutritional information per serving: Kcal: 152, Protein: 4.2g, Carbs: 48.1g, Fats: 1.3g

37. Arugula Juice

Ingredients:

1 cup of fresh arugula

1 large lemon, peeled

1 large lime, peeled

1 large orange, peeled

1 large kiwi, peeled

1 small cucumber

Preparation:

Combine all ingredients in a juicer and process until juiced.

Transfer to serving glasses and serve immediately.

Nutritional information per serving: Kcal: 192, Protein: 3.1g, Carbs: 31.6g, Fats: 0.9g

38. Mango Juice

Ingredients:

1 large mango, peeled

1 large cucumber

½ cup of fresh spinach

2 oz of coconut, grated

Preparation:

Combine mango, cucumber, and spinach in a juicer and process until juiced.

Transfer to serving glasses and stir in the grated coconut.

Refrigerate for 1 hour before serving.

Nutritional information per serving: Kcal: 68, Protein: 1.9g, Carbs: 20.1g, Fats: 0.5g

39. Bok Choy Leek Juice

Ingredients:

1 medium-sized leek

1 small baby bok choy

¼ cup of fresh basil

1 large green apple, cored

2 large carrots

4-5 fresh kale leaves

Preparation:

Combine all ingredients in a juicer and process until juiced.

Transfer to serving glasses and refrigerate before use.

Nutritional information per serving: Kcal: 169, Protein: 2.3g, Carbs: 46.2g, Fats: 1.9g

SALAD RECIPES

1. **Strawberry Spinach Salad**

Ingredients:

4 oz strawberries, chopped

4 oz grapes

1 large cucumber, chunked

1 small red bell pepper, chopped

1 tbsp olive oil

½ whole lime, juiced

2 cups fresh spinach, chopped

1 tbsp sunflower seeds

1 tbsp fresh basil, chopped

Salt to taste

Preparation:

Rinse the strawberries under running water and drain. Remove the stems and chop into bite-sized pieces. Set aside.

Wash the cucumber and cut into small chunks. Set aside.

Wash the pepper and cut lengthwise in half. Remove the stem and seeds. Chop into small pieces and set aside.

In a small mixing bowl, combine olive oil, lime juice, and salt. Mix until combined and set aside.

Now, combine spinach, strawberries, grapes, cucumber, and red bell pepper in a large salad bowl. Drizzle with previously prepared dressing and top with sunflower seeds and basil.

Serve immediately.

Nutritional information per serving: Kcal: 347, Protein: 7g, Carbs: 50.9g, Fats: 17.1g

2. Spanish Tuna Steak Salad

Ingredients:

4 oz tuna steaks

2 medium-sized tomatoes, chopped

1 large cucumber, sliced

1 medium-sized purple onion, sliced

¼ cup green olives, pitted

2 eggs, hard-boiled

1 whole lime, sliced

2 tbsp olive oil

2 tsp red wine vinegar

½ tsp dried rosemary, ground

½ tsp dried thyme, ground

Salt and pepper to taste

Preparation:

Rinse the meat under running water and pat-dry with a kitchen paper. Transfer to a cutting board and cut into thin slices.

Preheat 1 tasblespoon of oil in a skillet over medium-high heat. Add tuna steaks and sprinkle with salt, pepper, thyme, and rosemary. Cook for 2-3 minutes on each side. Remove from the heat and set aside.

Place the egg in a deep pot and add water enough to cover. Bring to a boil and then cook for 10-13 minutes. Remove from the heat and transfer to a bowl with ice cold water. When chilled, peel and chop into small pieces.

Wash and prepare the vegetables.

In a small mixing bowl, combine the remaining olive oil, red wine vinegar, dried rosemary, dried thyme, salt, and pepper. Mix until combined and set aside.

Now, combine tomatoes, cucumber, purple onion, olives, and eggs in a large salad bowl. Drizzle with previously prepared dressing and top with tuna steaks.

Serve immediately.

Nutritional information per serving: Kcal: 347, Protein: 7g, Carbs: 50.9g, Fats: 17.1g

3. Broccoli Kale Salad

Ingredients:

2 cups broccoli, chopped

2 cups fresh kale, chopped

1 small onion, chopped

1 small cucumber, sliced

½ cup cherry tomatoes, halved

1 tbsp extra-virgin olive oil

½ tsp dried oregano, ground

½ tsp dried thyme, ground

½ tsp salt

¼ tsp black pepper, ground

Preparation:

Rinse the broccoli under cold running water and drain. Cut into bite-sized pieces and transfer to a large pot. Add water enough to cover and bring to a boil over medium-high heat. Cook for 5 minutes and remove from the heat. Drain well and set aside.

In a small bowl, combine olive oil, dried oregano, dried thyme, salt, and pepper. Mix until well combined and set aside.

Wash and prepare the remaining ingredients.

Now, combine kale, cherry tomatoes, onion, cucumber, and cooked broccoli in a large salad bowl. Drizzle with the dressing and serve.

Optionally, sprinkle all with some lemon or lime juice for some extra flavor.

Enjoy!

Nutritional information per serving: Kcal: 342, Protein: 12.8g, Carbs: 48.2g, Fats: 15.3g

4. Tomato Onion Salad with Citrus Dressing

Ingredients:

1 cup cherry tomatoes, halved

1 small cucumber, sliced

¼ cup Feta cheese, crumbled

1 small purple onion, chopped

5 green olives, pitted and chopped

1 whole lemon, juiced

2 tbsp orange juice, freshly squeezed

2 tbsp extra-virgin olive oil

1 tbsp balsamic vinegar

½ tsp dried oregano, ground

Salt and pepper to taste

Preparation:

In a small mixing bowl, combine lemon juice, orange juice, olive oil, balsamic vinegar, dried oregano, salt, and pepper. Mix until well combined and set aside.

Rinse the cherry tomatoes under running water and

remove the stems. Cut into halves and transfer to a large bowl.

Wash the cucumber and cut into thin slices. Add to the bowl and set aside.

Peel the onion and chop into small pieces. Transfer to a small colander and rinse under water. Transfer to the bowl with the remaining vegetables.

Add crumbled cheese and drizzle with previously prepared dressing. Mix until well combined and serve immediately.

Enjoy!

Nutritional information per serving: Kcal: 249, Protein: 5.2g, Carbs: 16.1g, Fats: 19.9g

5. Mango Berry Salad

Ingredients:

1 large mango, chopped

½ cup fresh strawberries, chopped

½ cup fresh blueberries

½ cup fresh raspberries

1 cup grapes

1 medium-sized apple, chopped

1 large orange, peeled and wedged

3 tbsp fresh orange juice

1 tsp lemon zest, freshly grated

2 tsp liquid stevia

Preparation:

Peel the mango and remove the pit. Chop into bite-sized pieces and set aside.

In a large colander, combine strawberries, blueberries, and raspberries. Rinse under running water and drain. Remove the stems from the strawberries and chop into bite-sized pieces.

Wash the apple and cut lengthwise in half. Remove the core and cut into small pieces.

Peel the orange and divide into wedges. Cut each wedge in half and set aside.

In a small mixing bolw, combine orange juice, lemon zest, and stevia. Mix until combined and set aside.

Mix fruit in a large salad bowl and drizzle with previously prepared dressing. Toss to combine and chil in the refrigerator for 20 minutes before serving.

Enjoy!

Nutritional information per serving: Kcal: 292, Protein: 3.9g, Carbs: 73.6g, Fats: 1.6g

6. Asparagus Dijon Salad

Ingredients:

10 oz fresh asparagus, trimmed and chopped

½ cup cherry tomatoes, chopped

¼ cup ricotta cheese, crumbled

1 tbsp walnuts, finely chopped

1 garlic clove, finely chopped

1 tbsp olive oil

2 tbsp balsamic vinegar

2 tsp Dijon mustard

Salt and pepper to taste

Preparation:

Rinse the asparagus under running water and drain. Transfer to a cutting board and trim off the woody ends. Chop into bite-sized pieces and transfer to a deep pot. Add water enough to cover and bring to a boil over medium-high heat. Cook for 3 minutes and remove from the heat. Drain and set aside.

Wash the tomatoes and trim off the stems. Chop into small

pieces and set aside.

In a small mixing bowl, combine finely chopped garlic, olive oil, balsamic vinegar, Dijon mustard, salt, and pepper. Mix until well combined.

In a large salad bowl, combine asparagus, tomatoes, and ricotta cheese. Drizzle with previously prepared dressing. Sprinkle with walnuts and toss until combined.

Serve immediately.

Nutritional information per serving: Kcal: 344, Protein: 16.6g, Carbs: 20.3g, Fats: 24.4g

7. Pineapple Chicken Salad

Ingredients:

1 cup pineapple, chunked

6 oz chicken breast, skinless and boneless

2 cups fresh baby spinach

1 small purple onion, chopped

¼ cup Mozzarella cheese, sliced

2 tbsp avocado oil

2 tbsp cider vinegar

1 garlic clove, minced

¼ tsp cayenne pepper

Salt

Preparation:

Rinse the chicken under running water and pat-dry with a kitchen paper. Transfer to a cutting board and cut into bite-sized pieces. Transfer to a bowl and sprinkle with salt and cayenne pepper. Mix well with your hands and set aside.

Preheat one tablespoon of avocado oil in a skillet over

medium-high heat. Add chicken and cook for 5 minutes, stirring ocassionally. Remove from the heat and set aside.

Using a sharp knife, remove the top of a pineapple. Carefully peel and cut into 1-inch thick rings. Now, chop into bite-sized pieces and fill the measuring cup. Reserve the rest in the refrigerator.

Rinse the spinach under running water. Drain and transfer to a large salad bowl. Add pineapple, chopped onion, and cheese.

In a small mixing bowl, combine the remaining avocado oil, vinegar, and minced garlic. Mix until combined and drizzle over the salad. Stir once and top with chicken.

Serve immediately.

Nutritional information per serving: Kcal: 194, Protein: 21g, Carbs: 16.9g, Fats: 4.9g

8. Watermelon Cheese Salad

Ingredients:

4 cups watermelon, cut into chunks

1 cup Mozzarella cheese, sliced

1 cup baby spinach

1 tbsp fresh basil, finely chopped

½ tsp sea salt

½ tsp black pepper, ground

2 tbsp extra-virgin olive oil

1 tsp balsamic vinegar

Preparation:

Cut the watermelon in half. Cut and peel 3-4 large wedges. Chop into small chunks and remove the pits. Fill the measuring cups and reserve the rest in the refrigerator.

Rinse the baby spinach under running water using a colander. Drain and place in a large salad bowl.

Add watermelon chunks to the bowl along with mozzarella cheese. Sprinkle with salt, pepper, and basil.

Drizzle with olive oil and balsamic vinegar. Toss to combine and serve immediately.

Nutritional information per serving: Kcal: 257, Protein: 6.3g, Carbs: 24.3g, Fats: 17g

9. Broccoli Carrot Salad with Almonds

Ingredients:

3 cups broccoli, chopped

2 large carrots, shredded

½ small red onion, chopped

2 tbsp dried cranberries

2 tbsp almonds, roughly chopped

2 tbsp lemon juice, freshly squeezed

Salt and pepper to taste

Preparation:

Rinse the broccoli under running water using a large colander. Drain and chop into bite-sized pieces. Transfer to a large saucepan and cover with water. Add a pinch of salt and bring to a boil over medium-high heat. Cook for 2-3 minutes. Remove from the heat and transfer to a colander using a slotted spoon. Rinse under cold water and set aside.

Wash and prepare the remaining vegetables.

Now, in a large salad bowl, combine broccoli, carrots, and onion. Drizze with fresh lemon juice and stir until combined.

Top with cranberries and almonds and serve immediately.

Nutritional information per serving: Kcal: 250, Protein: 12g, Carbs: 40g, Fats: 7.1g

10. Bean Avocado Salad

Ingredients:

1 cup black beans, soaked overnight

1 large bell pepper, chopped

½ ripe avocado, sliced

1 small onion, chopped

1 tbsp extra-virgin olive oil

1 whole lime, juiced

¼ tsp cumin powder

1 tbsp spring onions, chopped

¼ tsp cayenne pepper, ground

Preparation:

Drain the beans and rinse under running water. Transfer to a deep pot and cover with 2 cups of water. Bring to a boil over medium-high heat. Cook for 20-25 minutes. Remove from the heat and drain well. Set aside.

Cut the bell pepper in half. Remove the stem and seeds. Rinse once and chop into bite-sized pieces. Set aside.

Peel the avocado and cut in half. Remove the pit and cut one half into bite-sized pieces. Reserve the rest in the refrigerator.

In a large salad bowl, combine beans, bell pepper, avocado, and chopped onion. Sprinkle with olive oil, lime juice, cumin powder, and cayenne pepper. Stir until well combined and sprinkle with spring onions before serving.

Nutritional information per serving: Kcal: 353, Protein: 15.4g, Carbs: 48.7g, Fats: 12.3g

11. Quinoa Tomato Salad

Ingredients:

1 cup quinoa

2 cups cherry tomatoes, chopped

1 medium-sized cucumber, sliced

1 small red onion, chopped

¼ cup cottage cheese, crumbled

1 tbsp fresh parsley, finely chopped

2 tbsp extra-virgin olive oil

2 tsp red wine vinegar

½ tsp garlic powder

½ tsp smoked paprika, ground

½ tsp dried oregano, ground

Salt and pepper to taste

Preparation:

Place the quinoa in a large colander and rinse under running water. Drain and transfer to a heavy-bottomed pot. Add 2 cups of water and bring to a boil over medium-high heat. Reduce the heat to low and simmer for 10-15 minutes, or until all the liquid has been absorbed. Remove from the heat and fluff with a fork.

In a mixing bowl, combine olive oil, red wine vinegar, garlic powder, smoked paprika, oregano, salt, and pepper. Mix until well incorporated and set aside.

In a large salad bowl, combine quinoa, tomatoes, cucumber, and onion. Drizzle with previously prepared dressing and toss to combine.

Serve immediately.

Nutritional information per serving: Kcal: 267, Protein: 9.6g, Carbs: 36.2g, Fats: 10.2g

12. Shrimp Potato Salad

Ingredients:

6 oz shrimps, cleaned and deveined

2 medium-sized potatoes, chopped

1 medium-sized tomato, chopped

1 small onion, sliced

1 garlic clove, minced

2 tbsp olive oil

½ whole lime, juiced

1 tbsp fresh cilantro, finely chopped

1 tsp Dijon mustard

Salt and pepper to taste

Preparation:

In a small mixing bowl, combine garlic, olive oil, lime juice, cilantro, Dijon mustard, salt, and pepper. Mix until combined and set aside.

Pour 3 cups of water in a deep pot. Bring to a boil over medium-high heat. Place the shrimps in a steam basked and place on top of the pot. Make sure that the shrimps are not submerged. Sprinkle with some salt and steam for 10 minutes, or until pink. Remove the basket from the pot and set aside.

Peel the potatoes and cut into small chunks.Rinse and transfer to a heavy-bottomed pot. Add water enough to cover and bring to a boil over medium-high heat. Cook until fork-tender and remove from the heat. Drain and set aside.

Now, combine potatoes, tomato, and onion in a large salad bowl. Top with shrimps and drizzle with previously prepared dressing.

Serve cold.

Nutritional information per serving: Kcal: 265, Protein: 16.1g, Carbs: 27.4g, Fats: 10.6g

13. Steamed Salmon Caprese Salad

Ingredients:

6 oz salmon fillets, cut into 1-inch thick slices

2 garlic cloves, crushed

1 cup cherry tomatoes, halved

2 cups Iceberg lettuce, torn

1 tbsp fresh basil, finely chopped

2 tbsp extra-virgin olive oil

2 tbsp Parmesan cheese, grated

1 tbsp white wine vinegar

½ tsp dried thyme, ground

Salt and pepper to taste

Preparation:

Rinse the salmon fillet under running water and pat-dry with a kitchen paper. Transfer to a cutting board and cut into 1-inch thick slices. Set aside.

Bring 2 cups of water to a boil in a deep pot. Place the salmon slices in a steam basket and sprinkle with some salt and thyme. Place the basket on top of the pot and cook for 10 minutes, or until set. Remove the basket from the pot and transfer the salmon to a plate. Cover with aluminum foil and set aside.

In a small mixing bowl, combine garlic, basil, olive oil, cheese, white wine vinegar, salt, and pepper. Mix until combined and set aside.

Rinse the lettuce under running water and drain. Torn into small pieces and place in a salad bowl. Add tomatoes and drizzle all with the previously prepared dressing. Toss to combine and top with salmon slices.

Serve immediately.

Nutritional information per serving: Kcal: 308, Protein: 22.3g, Carbs: 6.9g, Fats: 22.6g

14. Greek Skewer Salad with Marinated Feta

Ingredients:

1 cup Feta cheese, cut into bite-sized cubes

1 cup cherry tomatoes, whole

1 small cucumber, cut into bite-sized chunks

¼ cup black olives, pitted

1 garlic clove, minced

1 tbsp lime juice, freshly squeezed

2 tbsp olive oil

1 tsp fresh dill, finely chopped

1 tbsp fresh parsley, finely chopped

Salt and pepper

Preparation:

First, prepare the marinade for the Feta cheese. In a mixing bowl, combine olive oil, dill, parsley, lime juice, salt, and pepper. Mix until combined and add Feta cheese. Mix until all the cheese cubes are evenly coated. Refrigerate for 20 minutes.

Wash and prepare the vegetables.

Now, assemble the skewers. Layer cherry tomatoes, olives, cucumber, and marinated Feta cheese. Repeat the process with the remaining ingredients.

Serve immediately.

Nutritional information per serving: Kcal: 254, Protein: 8.6g, Carbs: 9.3g, Fats: 21.4g

15. Chicken Wrap Salad with Pecans

Ingredients:

4 oz chicken breast, skinless and boneless

½ cup Greek yogurt

1 tsp Dijon mustard

½ whole lemon, juiced

1 tbsp fresh dill, finely chopped

½ cup green grapes

¼ cup toasted pecans

½ cup spring onions, chopped

1 Romaine lettuce head

½ tsp Italian seasoning

Salt and pepper

Preparation:

In a mixing bowl, combine Greek yogurt, Dijon mustard, lemon juice, dill, salt, and pepper. Mix until combined and set aside.

Rinse the chicken under running water and pat-dry with a

kitchen paper. Transfer to a cutting board and cut into bite-sized pieces.

Preheat the oil in a saucepan over medium-high heat. Add chicken and sprinkle with Italian seasoning and salt. Cook for 5 minutes, or until golden brown. Remove from the heat and add to the bowl yogurt mixture.

Add all the remaining ingredients and mix until combined.

Spoon the mixture onto lettuce leaves and wrap. Secure the wraps with a toothpick and serve immediately.

Nutritional information per serving: Kcal: 169, Protein: 19g, Carbs: 14g, Fats: 4.6g

16. Kale Quinoa Salad with Sesame

Ingredients:

½ cup red quinoa

3 cups fresh kale, chopped

1 small purple onion, chopped

1 tbsp sesame seeds, toasted

¼ cup fresh cilantro, chopped

1 tbsp sesame oil

1 tbsp red wine vinegar

2 tbsp extra-virgin olive oil

Salt and pepper

Preparation:

Rinse the quinoa under running water and drain using a large colander. Place in a deep pot and add 1 cup of water. Bring to a boil over medium-high heat. Reduce the heat to low and simmer for 10-12 minutes, or until all the liquid has been absorbed. Fluff with a fork and set aside.

Place the kale in a colander and rinse thoroughly under running water. Drain and chop into small pieces.

In a large salad bowl, combine quinoa, kale, and onion.

In a small bowl, combine sesame oil, red wine vinegar, olive oil, salt, and pepper. Mix until well combined and drizzle over previously prepared salad. Toss to combine and sprinkle with toasted sesame seeds just before the serving.

Enjoy!

Nutritional information per serving: Kcal: 285, Protein: 6.8g, Carbs: 28.2g, Fats: 17.1g

17. Orecchiette Salad with Basil

Ingredients:

8 oz orecchiette pasta

1 tbsp fresh basil, finely chopped

2 tbsp sour cream

2 tbsp Feta cheese, crumbled

½ tsp dried rosemary, ground

2 tbsp olive oil

½ tsp dried oregano, ground

Salt and pepper

Preparation:

Place the pasta in deep pot and add water enough to cover. Bring to a boil over medium-high heat. Sprinkle with some salt and cook for 10-12 minutes, or until set. Remove from the heat and drain well. Rinse under cold running water and set aside.

In a food processor, combine fresh basil, sour cream, Feta cheese, rosemary, olive oil, oregano, salt, and pepper. Pulse until smooth.

Transfer the pasta to a salad bowl and drizzle with previously blended sauce mixture. Garnish with some basil and serve immediately.

Enjoy!

Nutritional information per serving: Kcal: 385, Protein: 10.7g, Carbs: 56.3g, Fats: 13.8g

18. Green Beans Salad with Eggs

Ingredients:

6 oz green beans, chopped

1 large egg, hard-boiled

1 cup cherry tomatoes, chopped

2 cups Romaine lettuce, chopped

¼ cup green olives

1 tbsp Parmesan cheese

1 tsp Dijon mustard

2 tbsp olive oil

2 tsp white wine vinegar

Salt and pepper to taste

Preparation:

Pour 3 cups of water in a saucepan and bring to a boil over medium-high heat. Add chopped green beans and cook for 2 minutes. Remove from the heat and rinse under cold running water immediately. Transfer to a paper-towel lined plate and pat-dry.

Now, place egg in the pot and water enough to cover. Bring to a boil and cook for 10 minutes. Remove from the heat and transfer to the prepared ice cold water bath. When chilled, peel and cut into slices. Set aside.

In a mixing bowl, combine Dijon mustard, olive oil, white wine vinegar, salt, and pepper. Mix until well incorporated and set aside.

Wash and prepare the remaining ingredients.

Combined beans, eggs, tomatoes, and lettuce in a salad bowl. Drizzle with previously prepared dressing and toss to combine. Finally, sprinkle with parmesan cheese.

Enjoy!

Nutritional information per serving: Kcal: 235, Protein: 6.3g, Carbs: 13.3g, Fats: 19.1g

19. Mackerel Salad

Ingredients:

4 oz mackerel fillets, skinless and boneless

2 cups Iceberg lettuce, chopped

1 medium-sized cucumber, sliced

1 whole lemon, juiced

1 garlic clove, minced

¼ cup sour cream

½ tsp dried thyme, ground

½ tsp dried rosemary, ground

1 tsp Dijon mustard

Salt and pepper

Preparation:

Rinse the fish fillets under running water and pat dry with a kitchen paper. Transfer to a cutting board and cut into small chunks. Sprinkle with some salt and set aside.

Pour 2 cups of water in a deep pot. Bring to a boil over high heat. Place the fish in a steam basket and place on top of the pot. Make sure that the fish doesn't touch the water. Steam until tender and flaky. Remove from the heat and set aside.

In a food processor, combine lemon juice, garlic clove, sour cream, thyme, rosemary, Dijon mustard, salt, and pepper. Pulse until smooth. Set aside.

In a salad bowl, combine lettuce and cucumber. Top with fish and drizzle with previously prepared sauce.

Serve immediately.

Nutritional information per serving: Kcal: 246, Protein: 15.9g, Carbs: 9.3g, Fats: 16.6g

20. Steak Salad with Caramelized Onions

Ingredients:

1 lb veal steak, cut into thin strips

1 large red onion, sliced

1 tbsp balsamic vinegar

2 tbsp olive oil

2 cups baby arugula, chopped

½ cup plum tomatoes, chopped

½ tsp dried oregano, ground

½ tsp dried thyme, ground

Salt and pepper

Preparation:

Rinse the meat under running water and pat-dry with a kitchen paper. Rub with some salt and pepper and set aside.

In a small saucepan, add balsamic vinegar and 1 tablespoon of olive oil. Heat up over medium-high heat. Add onions and cook for 5 minutes, stirring occasionally. Remove the onions to a plate and add steak. Cook for 3 minutes on each side for medium-rare. Transfer to a cutting board and cut into thin strips. Set aside.

Wash and prepare the remaining ingredients.

In a mixing bowl, combine the remaining olive oil, oregano, thyme, salt, and pepper. Mix until combined.

In a salad bowl, combine baby arugula and plum tomatoes. Drizzle with previously prepared dressing. Toss to combine and then top with steak strips. Top all with caramelized onion mixture and serve immediately.

Nutritional information per serving: Kcal: 283, Protein: 30.8g, Carbs: 5.3g, Fats: 15.1g

21. Steak Salad with Caramelized Onions

Ingredients:

1 lb veal steak, cut into thin strips

1 large red onion, sliced

1 tbsp balsamic vinegar

2 tbsp olive oil

2 cups baby arugula, chopped

½ cup plum tomatoes, chopped

½ tsp dried oregano, ground

½ tsp dried thyme, ground

Salt and pepper

Preparation:

Rinse the meat under running water and pat-dry with a kitchen paper. Rub with some salt and pepper and set aside.

In a small saucepan, add balsamic vinegar and 1 tablespoon of olive oil. Heat up over medium-high heat. Add onions and cook for 5 minutes, stirring occasionally. Remove the onions to a plate and add steak. Cook for 3 minutes on each side for medium-rare. Transfer to a cutting board and cut into thin strips. Set aside.

Wash and prepare the remaining ingredients.

In a mixing bowl, combine the remaining olive oil, oregano, thyme, salt, and pepper. Mix until combined.

In a salad bowl, combine baby arugula and plum tomatoes. Drizzle with previously prepared dressing. Toss to combine and then top with steak strips. Top all with caramelized onion mixture and serve immediately.

Nutritional information per serving: Kcal: 283, Protein: 30.8g, Carbs: 5.3g, Fats: 15.1g

22. Shrimp Avocado Salad with Mango

Ingredients:

10 oz shrimps, cleaned and deveined

1 ripe avocado, sliced

1 ripe mango, chopped

1 whole lime, juiced

2 cups fresh arugula, torn

1 small purple onion, diced

2 tbsp extra-virgin olive oil

¼ tsp cumin powder

Salt and pepper

Preparation:

Pour 2 cups of water in a deep pot. Bring to a boil over medium-high heat. Place the shrimps in a steam basket and sprinkle with some salt. Place the basket on top of the pot and cook for 5-8 minutes. Remove the basket from the pot and set aside.

In a small bowl, combine olive oil, lime juice, cumin powder, and salt. Mix until combined and set aside.

Wash and prepare all the remaining fruit and vegetables.

Now, combine arugula, avocado, mango, and onion in a large salad bowl. Drizzle with previously prepared dressing and toss to combine. Top with shrimps and serve immediately.

Enjoy!

Nutritional information per serving: Kcal: 307, Protein: 18.3g, Carbs: 20g, Fats: 18.4g

23. Chickpea Tomato Salad with Spinach

Ingredients:

1 cup canned chickpeas, drained and rinsed

1 large cucumber, chopped

2 cups cherry tomatoes, chopped

½ ripe avocado, chopped

2 oz Feta cheese, crumbled

2 tbsp fresh parsley, finely chopped

2 tbsp extra-virgin olive oil

½ whole lemon, freshly juiced

1 tsp Dijon mustard

2 garlic cloves, minced

1 tbsp fresh basil, finely chopped

½ tsp dried oregano, ground

Salt

Preparation:

Place the chickpeas in a colander and rinse well under cold

running water. Drain well and transfer to a large salad bowl. Set aside.

Rinse the cherry tomatoes and remove the stems. Cut into bite-sized pieces and set aside.

Wash the cucumber and cut into small pieces. Set aside.

In a small mixing bowl, combine olive oil, lemon juice, Dijon mustard, garlic, basil, oregano, and salt. Mix until well combined.

Now, add tomatoes, cucumber, avocado, and cheese to the salad bowl. Drizzle all with previously prepared dressing and toss to combine.

Serve immediately.

Nutritional information per serving: Kcal: 254, Protein: 7.1g, Carbs: 24.1g, Fats: 16g

24. Creamy Cucumber Garlic Salad

Ingredients:

2 cups Greek yogurt

2 tbsp sour cream

1 large cucumber, finely chopped

2 garlic cloves, minced

½ tsp onion powder

2 tbsp olive oil

½ tsp dried thyme, ground

½ tsp dried rosemary, ground

½ tsp red pepper flakes

Salt

Preparation:

Wash the cucumber and cut into tiny pieces. Set aside.

In a food processor, combine garlic cloves, onion powder, dried thyme, rosemary, red pepper flakes, and salt. Pulse until smooth. Now, gradually add olive oil and pulse until all well incorporated.

In a large bowl, combine Greek yogurt and sour cream. Mix and add garlic mixture. Toss to combine and fill small serving bowls.

Refrigerate for 20 minutes before serving. Optionally, sprinkle with some finely chopped parsley.

Nutritional information per serving: Kcal: 328, Protein: 21.8g, Carbs: 15.9g, Fats: 20.8g

25. Spicy Tortilla Salad

Ingredients:

½ ripe avocado, chopped

1 large cucumber

1 medium-sized red bell pepper

1 Iceberg lettuce head, chopped

¼ cup canned black beans, drained and rinsed

½ cup Mozzarella cheese, sliced

1 whole wheat tortilla, chopped into bite-sized pieces

2 tbsp olive oil

1 whole lemon, juiced

½ tsp chili powder

¼ tsp smoked paprika, ground

½ tsp salt

½ tsp black pepper, ground

Preparation:

Wash the cucumber and cut lengthwise in half. Using a

teaspoon, scrape out the seeds from each half. Cut into thin slices and set aside.

Peel the avocado and cut in half. Remove the pit and cut into bite-sized pieces and set aside.

In a small bowl, combine olive oil, lemon, juice, chili powder, smoked paprika, salt, and pepper. Mix until combined and set aside.

Now, combine avocado, cucumber, black beans, lettuce, red bell pepper, tortilla, and cheese in a salad bowl. Drizzle with previously prepared dressing and toss to combine.

Serve immediately.

Nutritional information per serving: Kcal: 299, Protein: 8.5g, Carbs: 30.9g, Fats: 17.8g

26. Swiss Cheese Kale Salad with Eggs

Ingredients:

¼ cup Swiss cheese, thinly sliced

2 cups fresh kale, torn

1 large egg, hard-boiled

1 shallot, finely chopped

1 tsp Dijon mustard

½ tsp garlic powder

1 tbsp chives, finely chopped

Salt and pepper to taste

Preparation:

Place the eggs in a deep pot. Add water enough to cover and bring to a boil over medium-high heat. Cook for 10-12 minutes and remove from the heat. Drain and transfer to a bowl with ice cold water. Add a few ice cubes and let it sit for 5 minutes to chill. Peel and cut into thin wedges. Set aside.

Using a large colander, rinse the kale under running water and drain. Torn into small pieces and set aside.

In a small bowl, combine shallot, Dijon mustard, garlic, chives, salt, and pepper. Mix until combined and set aside.

In a large salad bowl, combine kale, eggs, and Swiss cheese. Drizzle with previously prepared dressing and toss to combine.

Serve immediately.

Nutritional information per serving: Kcal: 256, Protein: 18.4g, Carbs: 18.9g, Fats: 12.7g

27. Shrimp Taco Salad

Ingredients:

10 oz shrimps, cleaned and deveined

1 cup cherry tomatoes, halved

2 cups Romaine lettuce, chopped

2 tbsp corn kernels

1 tbsp olive oil

2 tbsp fresh cilantro, finely chopped

1 whole lime, juiced

1 tsp honey

½ tsp cumin powder

½ tsp smoked paprika

¼ tsp black pepper, ground

Salt

Preparation:

Pour 2 cups of water in a deep pot. Bring it to a boil over medium-high heat. Place the shrimps in a steam basket and put on top of the pot. Cook for 10 minutes. Remove the basket from the pot and set aside.

In a small mixing bowl, combine olive oil, lime juice, honey, cumin powder, smoked paprika, pepper, and salt. Mix until combined and set aside.

In a large mixing bowl, combine cherry tomatoes, lettuce, and corn. Top with shrimps and drizzle with previously prepared dressing. Toss to combine and sprinkle all with fresh cilantro before serving.

Enjoy!

Nutritional information per serving: Kcal: 256, Protein: 18.4g, Carbs: 18.9g, Fats: 12.7g

28. Ginger Salmon Salad

Ingredients:

6 oz smoked salmon, cut into thin slices

2 tsp fresh ginger, shredded

1 tbsp soy sauce

1 garlic clove, minced

1 tbsp sesame seeds

2 tbsp olive oil

1 tbsp white wine vinegar

2 cups baby spinach

1 large carrot, shredded

2 tbsp spring onions, chopped

½ tsp dried thyme, ground

Salt and pepper

Preparation:

In a small mixing bowl, combine ginger, soy sauce, garlic, sesame seeds, olive oil, white wine vinegar, thyme, salt, and pepper. Mix until well combined and set aside.

Place the spinach in a large colander. Rinse under running water and drain. Cut into bite-sized pieces and set aside.

Now, place the spinach on the bottom of your serving bowl and top with smoked salmon slices. Drizzle with previously prepared dressing and serve immediately.

Enjoy!

Nutritional information per serving: Kcal: 284, Protein: 18.4g, Carbs: 8.7g, Fats: 20.2g

29. Fusilli Salad with Balsamic Glaze

Ingredients:

10 oz fusilli pasta

1 cup cherry tomatoes

1 large yellow bell pepper, chopped

1 onion, sliced

2 tbsp extra-virgin olive oil

1 tbsp balsamic vinegar

1 garlic clove, crushed

½ tsp Italian seasoning

Salt and pepper

Preparation:

Place the pasta in a deep pot and add water enough water to cover. Sprinkle with some salt and bring to a boil over medium-high heat. Cook for 10-12 minutes. Remove from the heat and drain well. Transfer to a large colander and rinse under cold running water. Set aside.

In a small mixing bowl, combine olive oil balsamic vinegar, garlic, Italian seasoning, salt, and pepper. Mix until well combined.

In a large salad bowl, combine pasta, cherry tomatoes, yellow bell pepper, and onion. Drizzle all with previously prepared glaze and toss to combine.

Serve cold.

Nutritional information per serving: Kcal: 342, Protein: 10.2g, Carbs: 59.4g, Fats: 8.2g

30. Spicy Rice Taco Salad

Ingredients:

½ cup brown rice

½ cup tomatoes, chopped

1/4 cup canned black beans

½ ripe avocado, sliced

2 tbsp fresh cilantro, finely chopped

½ cup Cheddar cheese, shredded

1 cup Greek yogurt

2 tbsp olive oil

2 tsp honey

1 tbsp apple cider vinegar

1 whole lime, freshly juiced

½ Jalapeno pepper, diced

1 tsp Taco seasoning

Salt

Preparation:

Place the rice in a deep pot and add ¾ cup of water. Sprinkle with some salt and bring to a boil over medium-high heat. Reduce the heat to low and cook for 10-15 minutes, or until almost all the liquid has been absorbed.

In a mixing bowl, combine Greek yogurt, olive oil, honey, apple cider vinegar, lime juice, diced Jalapeno pepper, Taco seasoning, and salt. Mix until combined and set aside.

In a large salad bowl, combine tomatoes, black beans, and avocado. Drizzle with previously prepared dressing and sprinkle all with fresh cilantro. Optionally, garnish with some lime wedges before serving.

Enjoy!

Nutritional information per serving: Kcal: 313, Protein: 12.9g, Carbs: 26.5g, Fats: 18.2g

31. Zucchini Noodle Salad

Ingredients:

2 large zucchinis

½ cup Mozzarella cheese, sliced

½ cup cherry tomatoes, halved

1 tbsp fresh basil, finely chopped

1 tbsp balsamic vinegar

2 tbsp extra-virgin olive oil

½ tsp dried thyme, ground

½ tsp dried parsley, ground

Salt and pepper to taste

Preparation:

In a small mixing bowl, combine olive oil, balsamic vinegar, thyme, parsley, salt, and pepper. Mix until combined and set aside.

Wash the zucchinis and remove the top stem. Run through a spiralizer and transfer to a large bowl. Drizzle with previously prepared mixture and toss well. Cover the bowl with a plastic foil and let it marinate for 20 minutes.

Meanwhile, prepare the remaining ingredients.

In a large salad bowl, combine cheese, cherry tomatoes, and marinated zucchinis. Sprinkle all with some salt, pepper, and finely chopped basil leaves.

Serve immediately.

Nutritional information per serving: Kcal: 313, Protein: 12.9g, Carbs: 26.5g, Fats: 18.2g

32. Gala Spinach Salad

Ingredients:

2 cups fresh baby spinach

1 Gala apple, thinly sliced

¼ cup Feta cheese, crumbled

1 small purple onion, sliced

2 tbsp toasted almonds, sliced

2 tbsp olive oil

1 tbsp red wine vinegar

1 garlic clove, minced

1 tsp Dijon mustard

Salt and pepper to taste

Preparation:

Using a large colander, rinse the spinach under running water. Drain and chop into small pieces. Set aside.

Wash the apple and cut in half. Remove the core and cut into bite-sized pieces. Set aside.

In a small mixing bowl, combine olive oil, red wine vinegar, garlic, Dijon mustard, salt, and pepper. Mix until combined and set aside.

Now, in a large salad bowl, combine spinach, apple, cheese, and onion. Drizzle all with previously prepared dressing and top with toasted almonds before serving.

You can change the red wine vinegar with lemon or lime juice. However, it is completely optional.

Enjoy!

Nutritional information per serving: Kcal: 265, Protein: 5.5g, Carbs: 15.1g, Fats: 21.5g

33. Creamy Tuna Salad

Ingredients:

½ cup canned tuna, drained

1 small purple onion, diced

2 tbsp fresh parsley, finely chopped

2 tbsp corn, drained and rinsed

¼ cup black olives, pitted

1 small cucumber, diced

2 tbsp Greek yogurt

2 tbsp olive oil

½ tsp smoked paprika

Salt and pepper to taste

Preparation:

In a small mixing bowl, combine Greek yogurt, olive oil, smoked paprika, salt, and pepper. Mix until combined and set aside.

Rinse the corn under running water and drain. Set aside.

Peel the onion and finely chop into small pieces. Set aside.

Wash the cucumber and dice into small pieces. Set aside.

Place the tuna in a sieve and rinse under running water. Drain by pressing with a spoon. Transfer to a salad bowl and add finely chopped parsley, corn, and diced onion. Mix once and then drizzle with previously prepared dressing. Toss until well combined.

Optionally, spoon the mixture onto a lettuce leaves and serve.

Nutritional information per serving: Kcal: 267, Protein: 13g, Carbs: 26.5g, Fats: 14.5g

34. Stuffed Avocado Salad

Ingredients:

1 ripe avocado, halved

4 medium-sized shrimps, cleaned and deveined

¼ cup cherry tomatoes, chopped

1 tbsp canned corn, drained and rinsed

½ tsp dried rosemary, ground

¼ tsp dried thyme, ground

½ whole lemon, juiced

1 tbsp olive oil

¼ tsp black pepper, ground

¼ tsp sea salt

Preparation:

Cut the avocado into halves and remove the pit. Gently scoop out the inner flesh, leaving a thin layer on the sides. Set aside.

Pour 2 cups of water in a deep pot. Bring to a boil over medium-high heat. Meanwhile, place the shrimps into the steam basket. Place the basket on top of the pot and steam for 10 minutes, or until pink. Remove from the heat and set aside.

In a mixing bowl, combine cherry tomatoes, corn, rosemary, thyme, lemon juice, olive oil, pepper, and salt. Mix until combined and add shrimps. Mix again until all well incorporated.

Spoon the mixture into prepared avocado shells. Optionally, garnish with some fresh basil.

You can use the scooped avocado flesh and mix it into the salad. However, it's optional.

Enjoy!

Nutritional information per serving: Kcal: 389, Protein: 14.7g, Carbs: 25.1g, Fats: 28.4g

35. Strawberry Spinach Salad with Quinoa

Ingredients:

¼ cup white quinoa

2 cups strawberries, chopped

2 cups fresh spinach, torn

¼ cup Feta cheese, crumbled

2 tbsp toasted almonds

2 tbsp olive oil

1 tbsp balsamic vinegar

½ tsp dried parsley, ground

¼ tsp dried oregano, ground

Salt and pepper

Preparation:

Place the quinoa in a heavy-bottomed pot and add ½ cup of water. Bring to a boil over medium-high heat. Reduce the heat to low and simmer for 10-15 minutes. Remove from the heat and fluff with a fork. Set aside.

Rinse the strawberries using a large colander. Remove the

stems and chop into bite-sized pieces. Set aside.

Rinse the spinach under running water and drain. Chop into small pieces and set aside.

In a small mixing bowl, combine olive oil, balsamic vinegar, parsley, oregano, salt, and pepper. Mix until well combined and set aside.

In a large salad bowl, add quinoa, strawberries, spinach, and cheese. Drizzle with previously prepared dressing and toss to combine. Finally, top with toasted almonds and serve immediately.

Nutritional information per serving: Kcal: 337, Protein: 8.8g, Carbs: 28.1g, Fats: 22.8g

36. Skirt Steak Salad with Peaches

Ingredients:

6 oz lean skirt steak

2 cups fresh arugula, chopped

1 large peach, thinly sliced

¼ cup Feta cheese, chopped

1 garlic clove, minced

1 tbsp olive oil

2 tbsp balsamic vinegar

½ tsp salt

¼ tsp black pepper, ground

¼ tsp dried thyme, ground

1 whole lemon, juiced

Preparation:

In a small mixing bowl, combine garlic, 1 tablespoon of balsamic vinegar, and salt. Mix until combined. Brush the steak with this mixture and let it sit for 15 minutes on room temperature. This will allow the juices to penetrate into the meat.

Preheat the grill to high heat. Generously brush the meat with olive oil and grill for 3 minutes on each side for medium-rare. Remove from the grill and cut into thin slices. Set aside.

Combine lemon juice, the remaining balsamic vinegar, salt, pepper, and thyme in a small bowl. Mix until combined and set aside.

Rinse the arugula under running water. Drain and chop into small pieces. Transfer to a large salad bowl along with peach and cheese. Top with steak slices and drizzle all with previously prepared dressing.

Serve immediately.

Nutritional information per serving: Kcal: 325, Protein: 26.7g, Carbs: 9.4g, Fats: 19.9g

37. Kiwi Mango Salad with Chia

Ingredients:

3 whole kiwis, peeled

1 ripe mango, chopped

1 small Granny Smith's apple, cored

1 large orange, peeled

1 cup green grapes

½ cup fresh blueberries

½ cup fresh raspberries

1 cup fresh strawberries

2 tbsp lime juice, freshly squeezed

1 tbsp honey

1 tbsp chia seeds

Preparation:

Peel the kiwis and cut into thin rings. Set aside.

Wash the mango and cut in half, avoiding the pit in the middle. Holding mango vertically, trim off the remaining flesh of the pit. Peel the skin and cut into small chunks. Set aside.

Wash the apple and cut lengthwise in half. Remove the core and cut into bite-sized pieces.

In a large colander, combine grapes, blueberries, raspberries, and strawberries. Rinse under running water and drain. Remove the stems from grapes and strawberries, if any. Chop the strawberries into small pieces and set aside.

In a small mixing bowl, combine lime juice, honey, and chia seeds. Mix until combined and set aside.

In a large bowl, combine all the fruit and drizzle with the dressing. Toss to combine and refrigerate for 20 minutes before serving.

Enjoy!

Nutritional information per serving: Kcal: 290, Protein: 4.6g, Carbs: 69.6g, Fats: 3g

38. Avocado Shrimp Salad

Ingredients:

1 ripe avocado, chunked

6 oz fresh shrimps, cleaned and deveined

1 small Jalapeno pepper, finely chopped

1 garlic clove, minced

2 tbsp lime juice, freshly squeezed

1 tbsp fresh cilantro, finely chopped

2 tbsp olive oil

¼ tsp dried thyme, ground

½ tsp smoked paprika, ground

Salt and pepper to taste

Preparation:

Cut the avocado lengthwise in half. Remove the pit and cut into bite-sized chunks. Set aside.

Pour 2 cups of water in a deep pot. Bring to a boil over medium-high heat. Place the shrimps in a steam basket and place on top of the pot. Steam for 3 minutes and gently toss. Continue to steam for another 3 minutes. Remove from the heat and set aside.

In a small mixing bowl, combine jalapeno pepper, garlic, lime juice, olive oil, thyme, smoked paprika, salt, and pepper to taste. Mix until combined.

In a large salad bowl, combine avocado and shrimps. Drizzle with previously prepared dressing and toss to combine.

Serve immediately.

Nutritional information per serving: Kcal: 292, Protein: 14.4g, Carbs: 8.7g, Fats: 23.5g

39. Spinach Orzo Salad

Ingredients:

3 cups fresh spinach, chopped

½ cup orzo pasta

1 cup cherry tomatoes, chopped

1 large egg, hard-boiled

1 tbsp olive oil

1 tbsp lemon juice, freshly sqeezed

½ tsp Italian seasoning

¼ cup Feta cheese, crumbled

¼ tsp red pepper flakes

Preparation:

Using a large colander, rinse the spinach under running water. Remove the hard stems and chop into small pieces.

Pour 1 cup of water in a deep pot and bring to a boil over medium-high heat. Place the spinach in a steam basket and sprinkle with some salt. Steam for 3 minutes. Remove from the heat and set aside.

Place the pasta in a deep pot and cover with water. Bring to a boil over medium-high heat. Cook for 10 minutes and remove from the heat. Transfer to a colander and rinse under cold water. Set aside.

Place the egg in the pot and add water enough to cover. Bring to a boil over medium-high heat and cook for 10-12 minutes. Remove from the heat and transfer to a prepared ice cold water bath. Let it chill for 2-3 minutes and then peel. Cut into thin wedges and set aside.

In a small mixing bowl, combine, olive oil, lemon juice, Italian seasoning, and red pepper flakes. Mix until combined and set aside.

In a large salad bowl, combine spinach, orzo, cheese, cherry tomatoes, and egg. Drizzle all with previously prepared dressing and serve.

Nutritional information per serving: Kcal: 252, Protein: 10.5g, Carbs: 22.1g, Fats: 14.5g

40. Grilled Mushroom Salad with Greens

Ingredients:

1 cup button mushrooms, chopped

1 cup fresh kale, chopped

1 cup fresh broccoli, chopped

2 tbsp bean sprouts

1 large Roma tomato, chopped

1 tbsp olive oil

¼ tsp dried parsley, ground

¼ tsp black pepper, ground

½ tbsp red wine vinegar

Salt

Preparation:

Rinse well the mushrooms and place on a large pieces of paper towel. Wrap and pat-dry. Sprinkle with some salt and set aside.

Preheat the grill to medium-high. Brush the mushrooms with olive oil and place on a rack. Grill for 3-5 minutes, turning occasionally. Remove from the grill and set aside.

In a large colander, combine kale and broccoli. Rinse under running water and drain. Chop into bite-sized pieces and place in a steam basket. Pour 1 cup of water in a deep pot and bring to a boil. Place the basket on top of the pot and steam for 3 minutes. Remove from the pot and set aside.

In a small mixing bowl, combine red wine vinegar, salt, and pepper. Mix until combined and set aside.

In a large salad bowl, combine mushrooms, kale, broccoli, and tomato. Drizzle with previously prepared dressing and top with bean sprouts. Optionally, drizzle with some more olive oil before serving.

Enjoy!

Nutritional information per serving: Kcal: 249, Protein: 9.8g, Carbs: 25.7g, Fats: 15.1g

41. Swiss Chard Salad with Cashew Sauce

Ingredients:

2 cups Swiss chard, chopped

1 small red bell pepper, chopped

½ cup red cabbage, shredded

1 small purple onion, sliced

½ cup cashews

½ tsp Dijon mustard

1 tsp honey

1 whole lime, freshly juiced

Salt

Preparation:

In a small mixing bowl, combine cashews, Dijon mustard, honey, lime, and a pinch of salt. Add about ½ cup of water and let it sit for 10 minutes.

Meanwhile, place the Swiss chard into a large colander and rinse under running water. Drain and chop into small pieces.

Wash and prepare the remaining vegetables.

Now, transfer the cashew mixture to a food processor and pulse until smooth and creamy.

In a large salad bowl, combine Swiss chard, red bell pepper, red cabbage, and onion. Drizzle all with previously prepared cashew sauce and stir until well coated.

Optionally, garnish with some fresh, finely chopped parsley.

Nutritional information per serving: Kcal: 292, Protein: 7.2g, Carbs: 34.3g, Fats: 16.2g

42. Spicy Mixed Salad

Ingredients:

1 large cucumber, sliced

1 cup cherry tomatoes, chopped

1 large yellow bell pepper, chopped

1 cup fresh spinach, chopped

1 tbsp extra-virgin olive oil

1 tbsp flaxseed oil

1 tsp apple cider vinegar

½ tsp dried oregano, ground

¼ tsp garlic powder

¼ tsp curry powder

¼ tsp cayenne pepper

Salt

Preparation:

Wash the cucumber and cut into thick slices. Set aside.

Rinse the tomatoes and remove the stems. Cut into bite-sized pieces and set aside.

Wash the bell pepper and cut lengthwise in half. Remove the stem and seeds. Chop into small pieces and set aside.

Rinse the spinach under running water using a large colander. Drain and chop into small pieces. Set aside.

In a small mixing bowl, combine olive oil, flaxseed oil, apple cider vinegar, dried oregano, garlic powder, curry powder, cayenne pepper, and a pinch of salt. Mix until combined and set aside.

In a large salad bowl, combine cucumber, tomatoes, bell pepper, and spinach. Drizzle with previously prepared dressing and toss to combine.

Optionally, add some crumbled Feta cheese for an extra flavor.

Nutritional information per serving: Kcal: 191, Protein: 3g, Carbs: 14.8g, Fats: 14.7g

43. Chickpea Salad with Sumac Dressing

Ingredients:

½ cup chickpeas, soaked overnight

1 large tomato, chopped

1 small purple onion, diced

2 tbsp cottage cheese, crumbled

1 tbsp Italian parsley, finely chopped

¼ cup olives, pitted

1 garlic clove, crushed

2 tbsp extra-virgin olive oil

½ whole lime, juiced

1 tbsp scallions, chopped

1 tsp sumac

¼ tsp cumin powder

½ tsp smoked paprika, ground

¼ tsp red pepper flakes

Salt and pepper to taste

2 cups Romaine lettuce, roughly chopped

Preparation:

Drain and rinse the soaked chickpeas. Transfer to a deep pot and 1-1 ½ cup of water. Bring to a boil over medium-high heat. Reduce the heat to low and cook for about 45 minutes to 1 hour. If needed, add more water while cooking. When done, remove from the heat and drain. Set aside.

In a small mixing bowl, combine garlic, olive oil, lime juice, sumac, cumin powder, smoked paprika, red pepper flakes, salt, and pepper. Mix until well incorporated and set aside.

In a large salad bowl, combine cooked chickpeas, tomato, onion, cottage cheese, olives, and parsley. Drizzle all with previously prepared dressing and toss to combine. Refrigerate for 30 minutes.

Now, spread the lettuce over the serving plate and spoon the salad on top.

Serve immediately.

Nutritional information per serving: Kcal: 332, Protein: 11.2g, Carbs: 33.9g, Fats: 18.7g

44.   Grapefruit Arugula Salad

Ingredients:

3 grapefruits, peeled and wedged

3 cups fresh arugula, chopped

½ ripe avocado, chopped

1 tbsp sunflower seeds

1 tbsp almonds, chopped

2 tbsp avocado oil

1 tbsp white wine vinegar

1 whole lime, freshly juiced

1 tsp yellow mustard

1 tsp turmeric powder

1 tbsp nutritional yeast

Salt and pepper

Preparation:

In a small mixing bowl, combine avocado oil, white wine vinegar, lime juice, yellow mustard, turmeric powder, nutritional yeast, salt, and pepper. Mix until all well incorporated and set aside.

Place the arugula in a large colander and rinse under running water. Drain and chop into small pieces. Set aside.

Peel the grapefruits and divide into wedges. Cut each wedge in half and set aside.

Peel the avocado and cut lengthwise in half. Remove the pit and chop one half into bite-sized pieces. Reserve the rest in the refrigerator.

In a large salad bowl, combine arugula, grapefruit, and avocado. Drizzle all with previously prepared dressing and serve immediately.

Enjoy!

Nutritional information per serving: Kcal: 284, Protein: 6.4g, Carbs: 25.1g, Fats: 19.9g

45. Hokkaido Salad

Ingredients:

2 cups hokkaido pumpkin, cubed

2 cups fresh kale, chopped

½ cup Feta cheese, cubed

1 small onion, diced

1 garlic clove, minced

1 tbsp pumpkin seeds

1 tbsp avocado oil

1 tbsp hard goat's cheese, grated

Salt and pepper

Preparation:

Preheat the oven to 350 degrees. Line some parchment paper over a large baking sheet and set aside.

Cut the pumpkin in half and scoop out the seeds. Cut and peel 2 large wedges. Chop into bite-sized cubes and fill the measuring cup. Reserve the rest in the refrigerator. Spread the pumpkin over the prepared sheet and sprinkle with olive oil, salt, and pepper. Place it in the oven and roast for

20 minutes.

Meanwhile, prepare the remaining ingredients.

Rinse the kale under running water. Drain and remove the hard ribs. Chop into small pieces and set aside.

In a food processor, combine avocado oil, garlic, onion, pumpkin seeds, salt, and pepper. Pulse until smooth and well incorporated.

In a large salad bowl, combine pumpkin, kale, and cheese. Drizzle with previously prepared dressing and toss to combine.

Serve cold.

Nutritional information per serving: Kcal: 278, Protein: 12.6g, Carbs: 33.3g, Fats: 12.8g

46. Quinoa Bean Salad with Mango

Ingredients:

½ cup canned black beans, drained and rinsed

½ cup quinoa

1 ripe mango, chopped

1 small red bell pepper, diced

2 tbsp fresh parsley, finely chopped

½ whole lime, freshly juiced

2 tbsp olive oil

½ tsp black pepper

¼ tsp salt

Preparation:

Place the quinoa in a colander and rinse thoroughly under runnning water. Drain and transfer to a deep pot. Add 1 cup of water and bring to a boil over medium-high heat. Reduce the heat to low and cook for 10-15 minutes, or until all the liquid has been soaked up and evaporated. Stir once and remove from the heat. Set aside.

Rinse and drain the black beans and place in a large salad

bowl along with chopped mango, and bell pepper.

In a small mixing bowl, combine parlsey, lime, olive oil, black pepper, and salt. Mix until combined and drizzle over the salad.

Toss again to combine and serve immediately.

Nutritional information per serving: Kcal: 302, Protein: 7.9g, Carbs: 45g, Fats: 11.7g

47. Eastern Halloumi Salad with Beluga Lentils

Ingredients:

½ cup halloumi cheese

1 cup beluga lentils, soaked overnight

1 tbsp pine nuts

1 large cucumber, sliced

¼ cup black olives

1 tbsp fresh coriander, finely chopped

1 tbsp wild garlic, finely chopped

1 tbsp dried seaweed, chopped

1 whole lime, freshly juiced

Salt and pepper

Preparation:

Preheat a large saucepan over medium-high heat. Add cheese and fry for 3-4 minutes, or until golden brown and crispy. Remove from the heat and set aside.

Rinse and drain the lentils. Place in a deep bowl and add 2 cups of water. Bring to a boil over medium-high heat. Cook for 30 minutes and remove from the heat. Drain well and set aside.

In a large salad bowl, combine halloumi cheese, lentils, cucumber, and olives. Sprinkle all with lime juice, coriander, wild garlic, seaweed, salt, and pepper. Mix until well combined and top pine nuts before serving.

Nutritional information per serving: Kcal: 260, Protein: 15.2g, Carbs: 18.6g, Fats: 14.8g

48.   Roasted Beet Salad with Mixed Greens

Ingredients:

2 medium-sized beets, sliced

1 cup fresh spinach, chopped

1 cup fresh arugula, chopped

1 cup fresh kale, chopped

1 large orange, peeled and wedged

2 tbsp pumpkin seeds

1 whole lime, freshly squeezed

¼ cup pomegranate seeds

1 tsp Italian seasoning

¼ tsp garlic powder

1 tbsp apple cider vinegar

3 tbsp olive oil

Salt and pepper to taste

Preparation:

Preheat the oven to 400 degrees. Line some parchment

paper over a baking sheet and set aside.

Wash the beets and transfer to a cutting board. Using a sharp knife, trim off the green parts and cut into thin slices. Sprinkle with some salt and spread over the prepared baking sheet. Place it in the oven and roast for 35-40 minutes, or until fork-tender. Remove from the oven and set aside.

In a small mixing bowl, combine olive oil, lime juice, Italian seasoning, garlic pwder, apple cider vinegar, salt, and pepper. Mix until well combined and set aside.

Combine all greens in a large colander and rinse under running water. Drain well and chop into small pieces.

In a large salad bowl, place the greens and top with beets. Sprinkle all with previously prepared dressing and toss to combine.

Serve immediately.

Nutritional information per serving: Kcal: 239, Protein: 4.4g, Carbs: 20.2g, Fats: 17.4g

MEAL RECIPES

Breakfast Recipes

1. Banana Manuka honey smoothie

Ingredients:

1 cup of chilled apple juice

Handful of chopped spinach

1 banana, medium-sized

2 tsp of Manuka honey

grated ginger, to taste

Preparation:

Toss all the ingredients into your blender and turn it on. Keep blending till the banana and spinach are completely smooth. Your Manuka honey smoothie is ready!

Nutrition information per serving: Kcal: 238 Protein: 7.5g, Carbs: 35g, Fats: 5g

2. Apple muesli with goji berries and flax seeds

Ingredients:

1 cup rolled oats

½ cup dried goji berries

2 large apples

3 tablespoons Flax Seeds

3 tablespoons honey

1 ¼ cups coconut water

1 ¼ cups plain yogurt

2 tablespoons mint leaves

Himalayan crystal salt, to taste

Preparation:

Grate the apples into a large bowl. Put the yogurt, Goji berries, flax seeds, rolled oats, mint and coconut water in the bowl and mix well. Leave the mixture in the fridge overnight. Blend the salt and honey into the muesli and serve!

Nutrition information per serving: Kcal: 280 Protein: 4g, Carbs: 44.5, Fats: 6g

3. Organic Deli burrito with spinach

Ingredients

2 slices of organic deli meat

1 teaspoon of ghee

2 whole eggs

¼ cup of chopped spinach

Pinch of salt

2 tablespoons of minced bell pepper

1 small tomato, minced

Guacamole sauce and Fresh cilantro, for serving

Preparation:

Whisk the eggs and salt in a mixing bowl and set aside. In a pan, apply medium-high heat and add the ghee. Sauté the spinach, tomato and bell pepper for 3 minutes. Add the eggs and scramble the mixture with a spatula. When the scrambled egg is done, remove from heat and add into each sliced deli meat.

Roll the ham and secure the end with a toothpick. Brown the deli meat evenly on all sides and transfer to a serving plate. Serve warm with guacamole and cilantro.

Nutrition information per serving: Kcal: 300 Protein: 19g, Carbs: 75.5g, Fats: 20g

4. Cashews Porridge

Ingredients:

1 ripe yellow banana, sliced

2 cups of unsweetened coconut milk

½ tablespoon of cinnamon

½ cup chopped cashews

½ cup chopped almonds

½ cup chopped pecans

Pinch of salt

Preparation:

In a mixing bowl, place the nuts and pour in with just enough water to cover. Sprinkle with salt, cover bowl and soak overnight. Drain and rinse with running water. Transfer into a food processor together with the banana, coconut milk, and cinnamon. Process the ingredients until thick and smooth.

Place the mixture in a pan over medium-high heat. Cook for about 5 minutes, or until it reaches to a boil while stirring regularly. Portion into 4 individual serving bowls and serve with extra chopped nuts if desired.

Nutrition information per serving: Kcal: 300 Protein: 7.2g, Carbs: 17.5g, Fats: 25.5g

5. Cherry tomato omelet

Ingredients:

4 medium free-range whole eggs, beaten

½ cup cottage cheese

½ cup diced white onion

1 cup fresh spinach

6 pieces of cherry tomatoes, diced

1 tablespoon of olive oil

Salt and pepper, to taste

Preparation:

Add the oil in a skillet and apply with medium heat. Sauté the onions until soft and pour in the beaten eggs. Cook for about 3 minutes or until the bottom part is lightly brown.

Add the cheese, spinach and tomatoes on one side of the egg and season to taste with salt and pepper. Carefully lift the other side of the omelet and flip it over to cover the vegetables. Reduce the heat to low and cook for about 2 minutes.

Slide the omelet onto a serving plate and serve with extra

cheese on top.

Nutrition information per serving: Kcal: 140 Protein: 14g, Carbs: 3.5g, Fats: 8.5g

6. Almond meal pancakes

Ingredients:

1 cup almond flour

2 medium free-range whole eggs

½ cup water

½ teaspoon baking soda

¼ teaspoon salt

¼ teaspoon of sugar

2 ounces of ghee

Directions:

Combine together the flour, salt and baking soda in a mixing bowl and set aside. In a separate bowl, whisk together the eggs, sugar and 1 tablespoon of ghee until well combined. Pour the egg mixture into the bowl with the flour mixture and mix it thoroughly until smooth. If the batter mixture is too thick, add water and mix until the desired consistency is achieved. Cover the bowl with a cloth and let it sit for 15 minutes, set aside.

Add the remaining ghee into a pan and apply with medium-high heat. Once the ghee is hot, pour in enough pancake mixture just to cover the base of the pan. Cook until the bottom part is lightly browned and flip it over to cook the other side. Repeat the procedure with the remaining pancake mixture and place them on a serving platter.

Serve warm with your favorite spread, if desired.

Nutrition information per serving: Kcal: 149 Protein: 6.1g, Carbs: 4g, Fats: 13,5g

7. Shredded Coconut Blackberry Pudding with Chia and Pistachios

Ingredients:

1 cup of almond milk

½ teaspoon of almond extract

½ cup of crushed fresh blackberries

3 tablespoons of chia seeds

1 tablespoon of shredded coconut

¼ cup of chopped raw pistachios

Preparation:

Combine together the crushed blackberries, chia seeds, almond extract, almond milk and shredded coconut in a mixing bowl. Mix the ingredients well until well combined.

Cover the bowl with plastic wrap and refrigerate for at least 12 hours before serving.

Serve the blackberry pudding with chopped pistachios on top.

Nutrition information per serving: Kcal: 300 Protein: 19g, Carbs: 50.5g, Fats: 6.5g

8. Blueberry Breakfast Tortilla

Ingredients:

1 tablespoon of extra virgin olive oil

4 eggs, beaten

1 tablespoon of almond butter

Pinch of black pepper

1 teaspoon of ground cinnamon

½ cup of fresh blueberries

Preparation:

Whisk together the almond butter, eggs, cinnamon and pepper in a bowl and set aside.

In a skillet, apply medium heat and add the oil. Pour in the egg mixture and cook for 3 minutes without stirring. Top with blueberries and cover with lid. Reduce to low heat and cook for 6 to 8 minutes more.

Remove the lid, place a plate on top of the skillet and flip the skillet to remove the egg tortilla. Return the skillet to the stove, slide in the tortilla in the skillet to cook the other side. Cover and cook for 3 to 4 minutes more.

When the blueberry tortilla is done, slide into a serving plate and serve warm.

Nutrition information per serving: Kcal: 168 Protein: 6g, Carbs: 24.5g, Fats: 6g

9. Buckwheat with cranberries

Ingredients:

1 cup of fresh cranberries

1 cups of buckwheat groats

1 medium apple, peeled and cut into slices

1 cup of low - fat yogurt

3 egg whites

½ cup of maple syrup

Preparation:

Preheat the oven to 350 degrees. Spread the buckwheat groats over a baking sheet and toast for about 5-6 minutes. You want a nice lightly brown color.

Boil the cranberries over a high temperature. Cook until they burst. Add the toasted buckwheat groats, egg whites, and apple slices and stir well. Cook for another 7 minutes, or until the buckwheat groats are cooked. Stir in the maple syrup. Remove from the heat and let it stand for 10 minutes. Serve cold topped with yogurt.

Nutrition information per serving: Kcal: 158 Protein: 4g, Carbs: 22.5g, Fats: 4.5g

10. Apple and quinoa muesli with walnuts

Ingredients:

½ cup of ground walnuts

2 large apples

3 tbsp of flax seeds

3 tbsp of brown sugar

1 ¼ cups of coconut water

1 ¼ cups of yogurt

1 cup of quinoa

2 tablespoons of mint leaves

Preparation:

Wash and peel the apples. Cut them into bite - size pieces and place in a large bowl. Add yogurt, walnuts, flax seeds, quinoa seeds, mint and coconut water in the bowl and stir well. Leave the mixture in the fridge overnight.

Top with honey before serving.

Nutrition information per serving: Kcal: 215 Protein: 8.3g, Carbs: 24.4g, Fats: 10.5g

11. Frozen cream with blueberries

Ingredients:

1 cup of low fat cream

1 cup of fresh blueberries

¼ cup of skim milk

2 egg whites

1 tbsp of honey

1 tsp of brown sugar

Preparation:

Combine the ingredients in a large bowl. Beat well with a fork. Put it in a freezer for about 30 minutes. This creamy mixture goes perfectly with a gluten-free, buckwheat toast.

Nutrition information per serving: Kcal: 101 Protein: 2.5g, Carbs: 19.5g, Fats: 0g

12. Peanut butter oats

Ingredients:

1 cup of oats, cooked

1 cup of unsweetened almond milk

2 tbsp of organic peanut butter

1 tbsp of strawberry syrup

1 tsp of cinnamon

Preparation:

Place the ingredients in a bowl and stir well until you get a nice, smooth mixture. If necessary, add some water. Pour this mixture in a tall glasses and leave in the refrigerator overnight.

13. Egg and cheese sandwich with dry parsley

Ingredients:

4 eggs

1 cup of cottage cheese

1 tsp of dried parsley

8 thin slices of whole grain bread

salt to taste

Preparation:

Boil the eggs for 10 minutes. Allow to cool and peel them. Cut into thin slices – about 5-6 slices of each egg. Layer 1 tbsp of low-fat cottage cheese on top of the bread and top with the egg, sliced.

Nutrition information per serving: Kcal: 280 Protein: 14g, Carbs: 27g, Fats: 13g

14. Fried egg whites with cottage cheese

Ingredients:

4 eggs

1 cup of cottage cheese

¼ cup of skim milk

1 tbsp of olive oil

salt to taste

Preparation:

Remove the egg whites from yolks. Grease the frying pan with olive oil. Heat up over to medium-high heat. Whisk together egg whites, cottage cheese, and milk. Add some salt to taste. Fry for 3-4 minutes, stirring constantly.

Nutrition information per serving: Kcal: 360 Protein: 34g, Carbs: 12.5g, Fats: 17.5g

15. Feta and eggs toast

Ingredients:

4 slices of whole grain bread

3 eggs

1 cup of baby spinach, chopped

½ cup of feta cheese

2 tbsp of extra virgin olive oil

Preparation:

Beat the eggs with a fork in a bowl. Cut feta cheese into small cubes and add them to the bowl. Grease the frying pan with olive oil. Heat up over to medium-high heat and fry baby spinach for several minutes, stirring constantly. Add egg and feta mixture and fry for several more minutes.

Put the bread in the toaster for 2 minutes. Serve with egg, feta and spinach mixture.

Nutrition information per serving: Kcal: 317 Protein: 15.5g, Carbs: 20.5g, Fats: 19.5g

16. Spinach omelet

Ingredients:

4 eggs

1 cup of baby spinach leaves, chopped

1 tbsp of onion powder

¼ tsp of ground red pepper

¼ tsp of sea salt

1 tbsp of Parmesan cheese

1 tbsp of olive oil

Preparation:

Beat the eggs with a fork, in a large bowl. Add baby spinach and Parmesan cheese. Mix well. Season with onion powder, red pepper and sea salt.

Heat upIn a bowl, beat the eggs, and stir in the baby spinach and Parmesan cheese. Season with onion powder, nutmeg, salt, and pepper.

Heat up the olive oil over a medium heat. Add egg mixture and fry for 2-3 minutes.

Nutrition information per serving: Kcal: 215 Protein: 24g, Carbs: 3g, Fats: 14g

17. Quinoa cereal

Ingredients:

1 cup of quinoa cereal

1 cup of plums, cut in half and pitted

1 tbsp of sugar

2 tbsp of maple syrup

1 tbsp of coconut oil, melted

½ tsp of cinnamon, ground

1 tsp of vanilla extract

water

Preparation:

Put your plums in a large skillet and add enough water to cover them. Bring it to boil and cook for 10 minutes, or until tender. Remove from the heat and drain. Set aside.

Use the same skillet to boil 2 cups of water. Add quinoa cereals, sugar, maple syrup, coconut oil, cinnamon, and vanilla extract. Reduce the heat to minimum and cook until slightly thickened. This should take about 5 minutes. Remove from the heat and pour into bowls. Top with plums.

Nutrition information per serving: Kcal: 131 Protein: 4.4g, Carbs: 23g, Fats: 3g

18. Coconut bananas

Ingredients:

2 large bananas, sliced lengthwise

1 cup of coconut milk

1 tsp of coconut oil

1 tsp of coconut extract

2 tbsp of agave syrup

¼ tsp of cinnamon

Preparation:

Pour 1 cup of coconut milk in a small saucepan. Bring it to boil and stir in coconut oil, coconut extract, and agave syrup. Cook for one minute and remove from the heat. Allow it to cool for a while.

Pour this mixture on each banana slice and sprinkle with some cinnamon. Serve cold.

Nutrition information per serving: Kcal: 182 Protein: 2.6g, Carbs: 28.8g, Fats: 7.3g

19. Eggplant French toast

Ingredients:

1 large eggplant

3 eggs

¼ tsp of sea salt

1 tbsp of oil

½ tsp of cinnamon

Preparation:

Peel eggplant and cut lengthwise into slices. Sprinkle salt on each side of eggplant. Allow it to rest for few minutes. Rinse well and press gently to drain and extract any excess liquid.

Meanwhile, mix eggs with cinnamon in a large bowl. Heat up 1 tbsp of oil in frying pan over a high temperature.

Put your eggplant slices in egg mixture. Make few holes with a knife to allow the mixture to permeate the eggplant. Fry it until golden brown color, on each side. Serve your 'French toast' warm.

Nutrition information per serving: Kcal: 118 Protein: 4g, Carbs: 12g, Fats: 8g

20. Cottage cheese and banana pancakes

Ingredients:

1 cup of sliced banana

½ cup of rice fluor

½ cup of skim milk

½ cup of almond milk

3 tbsp of brown sugar

1 tsp of vanilla extract

1 egg

½ cup of low fat cream

non-fat cooking spray

Preparation:

Combine banana slices, rice flour, skim milk and almond milk in a bowl and mix with an electric mixer until smooth mixture. Cover it and let it stand for 15 minutes.

In another bowl, mix the cream with sugar vanilla extract and egg. Beat well with a fork, or even better with an electric mixer. You want to get a foamy mixture. Set aside.

Sprinkle some non-fat cooking spray on a frying pan. Use ¼ cup of banana mixture to make one pancake. Fry your pancakes for about 2-3 minutes on each side. This mixture should give you 8 pancakes.

Spread 1 tbsp of cheese mixture over each pancake and serve.

Nutrition information per serving: Kcal: 340 Protein: 22g, Carbs: 42g, Fats: 8.5g

Lunch Recipes

21. Ginger and chili chicken thighs

Ingredients:

2 pounds chicken thighs (skin and bone should be left on)

1 tablespoon chili powder

Fresh basil

Black pepper, freshly ground

Sea salt

16 ounces coconut water

1 tablespoon grated ginger, fresh

1 tablespoon coriander seeds

8 peeled and lightly smashed garlic cloves

Preparation:

Put the chicken thighs along with garlic in the slow cooker. Add rest of the spices, sprinkling them evenly over the chicken thighs. Pour the coconut water on the thighs and add the fresh basil. Cover the slow cooker and set the heat to low. You need to cook the thighs for around 8 to 10 hours before they are tender enough to eat. The liquid will also give off an enticing aroma when the ginger chili chicken is ready.

Nutrition information per serving: Kcal: 262 Protein: 26.6g, Carbs: 17.4g, Fats: 8g

22. Beef stew

Ingredients:

2 pounds grass-fed stew beef

1 tablespoon flax seed oil

6 ounces tomato paste

2 handfuls baby carrots

2 quartered sweet potatoes

1 chopped large yellow onion

1 handful fresh mushrooms

½ tablespoon salt

1 bay leaf

2 ½ cups beef broth

½ cup frozen green peas

1 teaspoon thyme

3 minced garlic cloves

Preparation:

Take a frying pan and set it over high heat. Heat up the oil and add the beef to it. Fry the beef on all sides until properly brown. You may have to use more oil depending on how long it takes for a side to brown. Once the beef is brown, transfer it to the slow cooker. In the same pan, fry the onions, turning the heat to medium. Cook the onions for around 5 minutes.

Pour about ½ cup of water and the tomato paste in the frying pan to scoop up any remaining bits of the beef and onions. After this, pour the mixture over the beef in a deep pot. Put in all the remaining ingredients and stir properly, especially if the liquid is thick. Cover the pot, set the heat to low and cook for about an hour. 15 minutes before taking it off, toss in the frozen green peas to give them enough time to melt and cook.

Nutrition information per serving: Kcal: 220 Protein: 12g, Carbs: 16g, Fats: 13.2g

23. Chili Stew

Ingredients:

1 pound ground beef

8 minced garlic cloves

1 teaspoon garlic powder

2 tablespoons olive oil

1 tablespoon cumin

3 tablespoons chili powder

2 cups sliced mushrooms

1 pound cubed stew beef

1 chopped medium zucchini

1 minced medium onion

28 ounces tomato sauce

½ cup pureed carrots

2 cups beef broth

Preparation:

Put the ground beef in a frying pan along with a little oil.

Set the heat to high and fry till the beef turns brown on all sides. Once browned, transfer the beef to the slow cooker. In the slow cooker, add the cumin, carrots, chili powder, beef broth, tomato sauce and garlic powder to the ground beef. Stir properly to mix the ingredients in.

Use the frying pan to sauté the onion, mushrooms, zucchini, and garlic. The purpose is to soften each vegetable. Move the vegetables from the frying pan to the slow cooker once soft. Place the stew beef in the pan along with olive oil and chili powder. Fry till the beef turns brown on all sides and then move to crock pot. Cover the slow cooker, turn the heat to low and cook for 5 to 8 hours.

Nutrition information per serving: Kcal: 170 Protein: 7g, Carbs: 21.7g, Fats: 6.6g

24. Nacho casserole

Ingredients:

1 pound of ground beef

1 small onion, peeled and chopped

1 cup of spicy red beans

½ cup of canned corn, cooked

½ cup of sugar-free tomato sauce

2 tbsp of taco seasoning mix

1 cup of cottage cheese

1 cup of chopped green onions

Preparation:

Cook ground beef over a medium-high temperature, stirring occasionally. This process should take about 30 minutes. Remove from heat and drain well. Cut into bite size pieces and combine with red beans, corn, tomato sauce and seasoning mix. Stir well and simmer over medium heat for about 10 minutes.

Preheat oven to 350 degrees. Pour half of this mixture into baking casserole pan. Top with cottage cheese and green onions and add the remaining beef mixture. Bake for about 25 minutes.

Nutrition information per serving: Kcal: 450 Protein: 32.8g, Carbs: 18.4g, Fats: 29g

25. Striped bass

Ingredients:

4 large striped bass

1 tablespoon olive oil

½ tsp of sea salt

¼ tsp of black pepper

1 cup cottage cheese

Preparation:

Combine oil salt and pepper. Use a kitchen brush to spread this mixture over fish. Grill fish over a medium-high temperature, on each side for about 5 minutes. Serve with cottage cheese.

Nutrition information per serving: Kcal: 154 Protein: 28g, Carbs: 5g, Fats: 8.3g

26. Green chicken

Ingredients:

3 pieces of chicken breast (about 1 pound)

2 cups of spinach, chopped

1 cup of low - fat yogurt

3 green peppers

3 chili peppers

2 small onions, chopped

1 tbsp of ground ginger

1 tsp of red pepper powder

4 tbsp of oil

salt to taste

Preparation:

Wash and pat dry the chicken using a kitchen paper. Chop into bite size pieces. Finely chop onion and peppers and set aside.

Heat up the oil in a large weasel. Add onions and peppers and sauté for few minutes. Now add chicken breast pieces, ground ginger, red pepper powder, and salt. Stir-fry for ten minutes, or until the chicken turns light brown.

Meanwhile, combine low fat yogurt with spinach in a food processor. Mix well for 30 seconds. Add this mixture to the weasel and fry until the spinach gets well mashed. Cover the weasel, remove from the heat and let it stand for about 10 minutes before serving.

Nutrition information per serving: Kcal: 380 Protein: 16g, Carbs: 54.5g, Fats: 12g

27. Chicken in mushroom sauce

Ingredients:

1 pound of chicken meat, skinless

2 tbsp of all - purpose flour

1 cup of button mushrooms

1 cup of green beans, cooked

¼ cup of chicken broth

½ tsp of sea salt

¼ tsp of black pepper

4 tbsp of olive oil

Preparation:

Wash and pat dry the chicken meat. In a large bowl, combine all - purpose flour with salt and pepper. Coat the chicken with the flour and set aside. Heat up the olive oil over a medium temperature and fry chicken meat for about 5 minutes on each side. Remove from the saucepan and transfer to a plate. In the same saucepan add chicken broth, green beans, and button mushrooms. Bring it to a boil and cook for 2-3 minutes. Return the chicken and cook for another 20 minutes, stirring occasionally, until the water evaporates. Serve warm.

Nutrition information per serving: Kcal: 290 Protein: 21g, Carbs: 36g, Fats: 7g

28. Red beans mix

Ingredients:

1 cup of red beans, canned and cooked

½ cup of green beans

½ cup of button mushrooms

1 cup of cottage cheese

1 cup of Greek yogurt

2 egg whites

2 tbsp of coconut oil

1 tsp of sea salt

Preparation:

Combine the ingredients in a food processor. Mix well for 30 seconds. Preheat the oven to 300 degrees. Coat the small baking dish with 2 tbsp of olive oil. Pour the red beans mixture in a baking dish and bake for about 10-15 minutes. You want to get a nice light brown color. Remove from the oven, let it stand for about 10 minutes and cut into 4 equal pieces. Serve warm.

Nutrition information per serving: Kcal: 193 Protein: 5.4g, Carbs: 23.6g, Fats: 10.2g

29. Greek style chicken

Ingredients:

4 pieces of chicken breast halves

1 cup of cottage cheese

½ cup of Greek yogurt

1 cup of chopped cucumber

1 cup of chopped lettuce

1 cup of cherry tomatoes

½ cup of chopped onions

5 garlic cloves

2 tbsp of fresh lemon juice

1 tbsp of dried oregano

½ tsp of red pepper

½ tsp of salt

2 tbsp of olive oil

6 whole-wheat pitas, cut into wedges

Preparation:

Wash and cut the meat into small pieces. Set aside.

Combine the cottage cheese, Greek yogurt, vegetables and spices in a food processor. Mix well for 30 seconds. Heat up the olive oil over a medium temperature. Fry chicken chops for about 20 minutes, stirring constantly. Add the vegetable mixture to the saucepan. Stir well and cook for another 10 minutes. Remove from the heat and shape this mixture into 6 equal parts. Serve with pitas.

Nutrition information per serving: Kcal: 498 Protein: 23.6g, Carbs: 23.5g, Fats: 24

30. Cottage cheese with fried vegetables

Ingredients:

½ cup of cottage cheese

1 small onion

1 small carrot

1 small tomato

2 medium red peppers

salt to taste

1 tbsp of olive oil

Preparation:

Wash and pat dry the vegetables using a kitchen paper. Cut into thin slices or strips. Heat up the olive oil over a medium temperature and fry the vegetables for about 10 minutes, stirring constantly. Add salt and mix well. You want to wait until the vegetables soften, then add cottage cheese. Stir well. Fry for another 2-3 minutes. Remove from the heat and serve.

Nutrition information per serving: Kcal: 122 Protein: 11.5g, Carbs: 8.5g, Fats: 5.5g

31. Green bean burritos

Ingredients:

1 cup of cooked green beans

1 pound of lean veal, chopped

1 cup of Cheddar

½ cup of chopped onions

1 tsp of ground red pepper

1 tsp of chili powder

6 whole grain tortillas

Preparation:

Combine the meat with ground red pepper, chili powder, and onions in a frying pan. Stir well for 15 minutes on a low temperature. Remove from the heat.

Mix Cheddar with green beans in a blender. Mix well for about 30 seconds. Add the cheese mixture to the meat. Divide this mixture into 6 equal pieces and spread over tortillas. Wrap and serve.

Nutrition information per serving: Kcal: 370 Protein: 15 g, Carbs: 55.5g, Fats: 11g

32. Roasted lentils

Ingredients:

½ cups of uncooked lentils

1 tbsp of salt

2 tbsp of olive oil

1 tsp of pepper

1 tsp of red chili powder

1 tsp of cinnamon powder

Preparation:

First, you want to cook lentils. Pour about 2 cups of water in a saucepan and bring it to boil. Add lentils and boil for about 15-20 minutes, until soft from inside and still hold their shape. Remove from the heat and rinse well with cold water. Drain your chia seeds and set aside.

Preheat the oven to 300 degrees. In a large bowl, coat the lentils with salt, olive oil, pepper, red chili powder and cinnamon. Spread the lentils over a medium sized baking dish and bake for about 20 minutes.

Prepared like this, lentils can be stored in the airtight container for about 15 days.

Nutrition information per serving: Kcal: 110 Protein: 8g, Carbs: 19g, Fats: 3.5g

33. Seafood Balls

Ingredients:

1½ pounds white fish

Sea salt

Black pepper, freshly ground

½ pound shrimp

½ lemon juice

1½ cups almond flour

2 tablespoons tartar sauce

½ cup water

3 tablespoons fresh parsley

3 eggs

Cooking fat

Preparation:

Use a food processor to make a paste combining 2 eggs, ½ cup almond flour, shrimps, white fish, parsley, and lemon juice, blending till the paste is smooth. Take a bowl, pour some water and break an egg into it. Whisk the two and create a mixture. In a separate bowl, put the remaining almond flour and add salt and pepper to it.

Take a larger bowl and mix the contents of all three bowls. Then, make small balls out of the batter you have created. Put the balls in the skillet and fry for about 15 minutes. Enjoy with tartar sauce.

Nutrition information per serving: Kcal: 101 Protein: 9.4g, Carbs: 10.2g, Fats: 3.7g

34. Cayenne Pepper Shrimps

Ingredients:

2 pounds peeled and deveined large shrimps

2 tablespoons lemon juice

Cayenne pepper

Black pepper

Sea salt

4 minced garlic cloves

3 tablespoons butter

2 tablespoons chopped fresh parsley

2 tablespoons cooking fat

Preparation:

Take a frying pan and put in the butter. Heat until the butter melts and then throw in the shrimps. Fry the shrimps till almost opaque in appearance. Move shrimps to the large pan and fry the garlic for a minute or two. Add the rest of the ingredients, along with the garlic, to the pan. Cover and cook for 20 minutes over a medium temperature.

Nutrition information per serving: Kcal: 162 Protein: 24.6g, Carbs: 1.7g, Fats: 6.2g

35. Warm chicken bowl

Ingredients:

28 ounces diced fire roasted tomatoes

12 boneless & skinless chicken thighs

1 tablespoon dried basil

8 ounces full - fat coconut milk

Salt & pepper

7 ounces tomato paste

3 chopped celery stalks

3 chopped carrots

2 tablespoons coconut oil

1 finely chopped onion

4 minced garlic cloves

½ container mushrooms

Preparation:

Pour coconut oil in a frying pan and put over high heat. Add the celery, onions, and carrots and fry for 5 to 10 minutes. Move them to the skillet and add tomato paste, basil, garlic, mushrooms and seasoning. Keep stirring the vegetables till they are completely covered by tomato sauce. At the same time, cut the chicken into small cubes to make it easier to eat.

Put the chicken in the skillet, pour the coconut oil over it and throw in the tomatoes. Stir the chicken in to ensure the ingredients and vegetables are properly mixed with it. Turn the heat to low and cook for about 30 minutes. The vegetables and chicken should be cooked through before you turn the heat off. Pour some coconut milk on top before serving!

Nutrition information per serving: Kcal: 189 Protein: 4.2g, Carbs: 25.1g, Fats: 8g

36. Autumn Soup

Ingredients:

3 sliced sweet potatoes

Salt

vanilla extract

2 sliced fennel bulbs

15 ounces pureed pumpkin

1 large onion sliced

coconut oil

pumpkin pie spice

50 ounces boiling water

Preparation:

In the crock pot, melt around 1 tablespoon of oil on high heat. Then, turn the heat to low and put in onion and fennel bulbs. Continue cooking till they are caramelized. Add the rest of the ingredients to the pot and continue cooking till the sweet potatoes are sour. Cook on low heat to get the best possible result. After the process is completed, blend the soup until it is smooth and then add salt to taste.

Nutrition information per serving: Kcal: 115 Protein: 8.2g, Carbs: 14.3g, Fats: 3.2g

37. Spanish chicken

Ingredients:

6 chicken thighs

Half a cauliflower head

salt

1 can of chopped tomatoes

½ pound Brussels sprouts

1 medium chorizo sausage

3 medium zucchinis

Preparation:

Take a frying pan and add some oil. Fry the chicken thighs, removing the skin if you want, until they turn golden brown. Remove the thighs from the frying pan and move to a large pot. Next, chop the sausage and fry for around 3 minutes. After frying, put it in the pot as well.

Slice the zucchinis and break the cauliflower into small florets and put them in the pot as well. Also, add the Brussels sprouts to the pot. Add salt and then pour the chopped tomatoes over the ingredients. Set the heat to low and cook for about an hour. Serve with a side of baby corn.

Nutrition information per serving: Kcal: 430 Protein: 34.8g, Carbs: 39.5g, Fats: 15g

38. Onion-mushrooms beef tips

Ingredients:

2 pounds of grass-fed beef stew meat, cubed

Salt and ground pepper, to taste

2 tablespoons of olive oil

2 cups of fresh white mushrooms

2 cups of beef stock

½ white onion, chopped

1 tablespoon minced garlic

Preparation:

Season the beef with salt and pepper and toss to coat it evenly with spices.

In a stew pot over medium-high heat, add the oil and brown the beef evenly on all sides. Stir in the garlic and onions, sauté for 2 minutes and add the mushrooms

Add the oil in the inner pot, press the sauté button and adjust to brown mode. Season beef with salt and pepper and brown evenly on all sides in the inner pot. Stir in the onions and garlic and sauté for about 1 minute and then add the mushrooms and the stock. Cover with lid, bring it to a boil and reduce to low heat. Simmer for about 30 minutes or until the meat is tender and cooked through.

Adjust the seasoning and transfer into a serving bowl. Serve immediately.

Nutrition information per serving: Kcal: 158 Protein: 18.8g, Carbs: 2.7g, Fats: 8g

39. Turkey in orange sauce

Ingredients:

2 tablespoons of extra virgin olive oil

1 pound of turkey breast slices

Salt and ground black pepper, to taste

1 cup of chicken stock

2 tablespoons of olive oil, for the sauce

2 packets of sugar

2 teaspoons grated orange zest

2 tablespoons of fresh orange, juiced

1 teaspoon of cayenne pepper

Preparation:

Season the slices of turkey evenly with salt and pepper on both sides. Heat up the olive oil over a medium heat. Brown the turkey meat on both sides and transfer to a plate. Set aside. Add the oil, orange zest, orange juice, cayenne and the stock in the same pan and cook until it reaches to a simmer. Return the turkey meat in the pan and baste with sauce.

Cover with lid, bring it to a boil and reduce heat to low. Simmer for 45 to 60 minutes or until the meat is tender and cooked through. If the sauce is not yet thick, cook further without the lid until the desired consistency is achieved.

Transfer the turkey meat to a serving platter, drizzle over with sauce and serve immediately.

Nutrition information per serving: Kcal: 123 Protein: 13.5g, Carbs: 16.8g, Fats: 2.8g

40. Thai beef curry

Ingredients:

2 pounds of beef chuck steak, sliced into thin strips

2 tablespoons of olive oil

2 tablespoons kaffir lime leaves, thinly sliced

1 cup unsweetened coconut milk

½ cup beef stock or water (optional)

3 tsp of sugar

1 teaspoon salt

¼ cup of Panang curry paste

Directions:

In a stew pot over medium-high heat, add 1 tablespoon of oil and fry the kaffir lime leaves briefly. Add in the curry paste, reduce to low heat and cook for about 3 minutes or until aromatic.

Add the meat and cook for 5 minutes while stirring occasionally. Stir in the stevia, and then pour in the stock and coconut milk. Briefly, stir to evenly distribute the ingredients and cover with lid. Bring it to a boil and reduce heat to low. Simmer for 30 to 35 minutes or until the beef is tender and cooked through.

Adjust taste and cook further to adjust the consistency of sauce.

Portion the beef curry into individual serving bowls or transfer into a serving bowl and serve immediately.

Nutrition information per serving: Kcal: 420 Protein: 20.5g, Carbs: 19.6g, Fats: 32.2g

Dinner Recipes

41. Grilled tuna steaks

Ingredients:

¼ cup of chopped fresh coriander leaves

3 garlic cloves, minced

2 tablespoons of lemon juice

½ cup olive oil

4 tuna steaks

½ teaspoon smoked paprika

½ teaspoon cumin, ground

½ teaspoon chili powder

Salt and black pepper

Preparation:

Add the coriander, garlic, paprika, cumin, chili powder and lemon juice in a food processor and pulse to combine. Gradually add in the oil and pulse the ingredients until a smooth mixture is achieved.

Transfer the mixture into a bowl, add the fish and gently toss to coat the fish evenly with sauce. Chill for at least 2 hours to allow the flavors to penetrate into the fish.

Remove the fish from the chiller and preheat the gas/charcoal grill. Lightly brush the grid with oil, place the fish and grill for about 3 to 4 minutes on each side.

Remove the fish from the grill, transfer to a serving plate and serve with lemon wedges or preferred sauce.

Nutrition information per serving: Kcal: 240 Protein: 53.5g, Carbs: 4g, Fats: 2g

42. Green bean burritos

Ingredients:

1 cup of cooked green beans

1 pound of lean ground beef

1 cup of cottage cheese

½ cup of chopped onions

1 tsp of ground red pepper

1 tsp of chili powder

6 whole grain tortillas

Preparation:

Cook up the meat and rinse it. Chop it into bite size pieces and put it back in the pan. Add ground red pepper, chili powder and onions. Stir well for 15 minutes. Remove from the heat.

Combine cottage cheese with green beans in a blender. Mix well for 30 seconds. Add the cheese mixture to the meat. Divide this mixture into 6 equal pieces and spread over tortillas. Wrap and serve.

Nutrition information per serving: Kcal: 310 Protein: 14.5g, Carbs: 45.2g, Fats: 8.3g

43. Egg and avocado puree

Ingredients:

4 eggs

1 cup of skim milk

½ avocado

Preparation:

Hard boil your eggs. Remove from the heat and allow it to cool. Peel and cut the eggs. Add a pinch of salt and leave in the refrigerator for about 30 minutes. Place in a blender. Cut avocado into small pieces and add to the blender. Add milk and blend for 30 minutes. This puree should be eaten right away.

Nutrition information per serving: Kcal: 205 Protein: 13.4g, Carbs: 5.7g, Fats: 13.9g

44. Walnut and strawberries salad

Ingredients:

½ cup of ground walnuts

2 cups of fresh strawberries

1 tbsp of strawberry syrup

2 tbsp of non - fat cream

1 tbsp of brown sugar

Preparation:

Wash and cut the strawberries into small pieces. Mix with ground walnuts in a bowl. In a separate bowl, combine strawberry syrup, non - fat cream and brown sugar. Beat well with a fork and use to top the salad.

Nutrition information per serving: Kcal: 131 Protein: 4.4g, Carbs: 23g, Fats: 3g

45. Ginger eggs

Ingredients:

3 eggs

2 tbsp of olive oil

1 tsp of grated ginger

1/5 tsp of pepper

¼ tsp of sea salt

Preparation:

Beat the eggs with a fork. Add ginger and pepper. Mix well and fry in olive oil for few minutes. Serve warm. Season with sea salt.

Nutrition information per serving: Kcal: 74 Protein: 2.4g, Carbs: 8.1g, Fats: 4.2g

46. Chia seeds pate

Ingredients:

½ cup of chia seeds powder

¼ cup of chia seeds

½ cup of cottage cheese

3-4 cloves of garlic

¼ cup of skim milk

1 tbsp of mustard

¼ tsp of salt

Preparation:

Chop the garlic and mix with mustard. In a large bowl, combine cottage cheese with skim milk, salt, chia seeds powder and chia seeds. Mix well and add garlic and mustard. Allow it to stand in the refrigerator for about an hour.

Nutrition information per serving: Kcal: 40 Protein: 2.6g, Carbs: 6.2g, Fats: 4.7g

47. Chicken salad recipe

Ingredients:

3 skinless, boneless chicken breast halves

1 cup of chopped lettuce

5 cherry tomatoes

2 tbsp of low fat cream

1 tbsp of olive oil

1 tsp of chopped parsley

1 tbsp of sunflower oil

1 tsp of minced chili pepper

1 tbsp of lemon juice

salt to taste

Preparation:

Cut the chicken breast halves into small cubes. Mix the sunflower oil, chopped parsley, minced chili pepper and lemon juice to make a marinade sauce. Put the chicken cubes on a baking sheet, sprinkle with chili marinade and bake at 350 degrees for about 30 minutes. Remove from the oven.

Meanwhile, mix cherry tomatoes with chopped lettuce and low fat cream. Add chicken cubes and season with salt and olive oil.

Nutrition information per serving: Kcal: 102 Protein: 9.8g, Carbs: 5.2g, Fats: 4.8g

48. Eggs and onions salad

Ingredients:

2 medium onions

4 boiled eggs

1 grated carrot

1 cup of chopped baby spinach

1 tbsp of grated fresh ginger

1 tbsp of lemon juice

1 tbsp of olive oil

1 tsp of ground turmeric

salt to taste

Preparation:

Peel and cut the onions. Salt it and leave it to stand for 15-20 minutes. Wash and squeeze, sprinkle some lemon juice over it and leave it. Meanwhile, boil the eggs for about 10 minutes, remove from heat, peel and cut into small cubes. Combine it with baby spinach, grated carrot and ginger. Add onions and season with olive oil, salt, and turmeric. Serve cold.

Nutrition information per serving: Kcal: 365 Protein: 36.4g, Carbs: 8.7g, Fats: 21.9g

49. Citrus peppered shrimps

Ingredients:

1 pound fresh large shrimps, peeled and deveined

1 organic lemon, juiced and zested

½ teaspoon black pepper, freshly ground to taste

½ teaspoon salt, or as needed to taste

½ teaspoon chili powder

1 tablespoon of extra light virgin olive oil

2 tablespoons chopped fresh parsley leaves

Preparation:

Combine together the lemon zest, lemon juice, salt, black pepper and chili powder in a large bowl and add in the shrimps. Toss to coat the shrimps with the marinade mixture and chill for at least 2 hours to marinate the shrimps.

In a wok or skillet over high heat, add the oil when the wok or skillet is very hot. Stir fry the shrimps for about 5 minutes or until opaque and thoroughly cooked.

Transfer to a serving platter, top with chopped parsley and

serve with lemon wedges if desired.

Nutrition information per serving: Kcal: 142 Protein: 20.3g, Carbs: 2.8g, Fats: 6.2g

50. Kale and tomato stuffed chicken breasts

Ingredients:

4 boneless (4 ounces each), skinless chicken breasts

1 to 2 tablespoons of olive oil

½ cup soft goat's cheese

½ cup of kale, minced

¼ cup sun-dried tomatoes, chopped finely

Salt and black pepper, to taste

Preparation:

Preheat an oven to a temperature of 400°F. Lightly coat a baking dish with oil and set aside.

Add ½ cup of water into a pan, apply medium-high heat and bring to a boil. Add the kale, dried tomatoes and ½ tablespoon of oil and cook until the kale is wilted and the tomatoes have softened. Season to taste with salt and pepper and remove the pan from heat.

Slice the each breast into flat and thin pieces or flattened by a mallet. Lay the flat chicken meats on a work surface and add 1 tablespoon of cheese on the center part. Portion the kale-tomato mixture into each flat chicken meat, place them on the bottom side of the meat and season to taste with salt and pepper.

Roll the chicken upwards to cover the stuffing. Insert a toothpick on the end part of the meat to secure the stuffing. Lightly brush the top part with oil and transfer into the greased baking dish.

Bake it in the oven for about 25 minutes or until the chicken is thoroughly cooked and nicely browned. Remove from the oven and let it rest for 10 minutes before slicing and serving.

Serve warm with tomato salsa if desired.

Nutrition information per serving: Kcal: 420 Protein: 23.2g, Carbs: 23.7g, Fats: 1.7g

51. Lemon-rosemary marinated grilled chicken

Ingredients:

4 chicken breasts (4 ounce each), deboned and halved

2 tablespoons of clarified butter

1 organic lemon, juiced and zested

2 teaspoons dried rosemary leaves

2 garlic cloves, minced

1 teaspoon crushed black pepper

½ teaspoon table salt

4 slices of lemon wedges, for serving

1 tablespoon of olive oil, for coating and greasing

Preparation:

Combine together the lemon juice, lemon zest, rosemary, garlic, salt and pepper in a mixing bowl and add in the chicken. Coat the chicken evenly with the marinade mixture and chill for at least 2 hours.

Preheat the gas or charcoal grill and lightly brush the cooking grids with oil. Place the chicken on the grid and grill for about 5 to 10 minutes on each side.

Combine the ghee and marinade mixture, and brush it evenly on all sides the chicken while grilling.

When the chicken is done, remove it from the grill and let it rest for 5 minutes. Transfer to a serving platter and serve warm with lemon wedges if desired.

Nutrition information per serving: Kcal: 274 Protein: 27.2g, Carbs: 4.3g, Fats: 17.1

52. Eggs with fried vegetables and chia seeds

Ingredients:

2 eggs

3 egg whites

1 small onion

1 small carrot

1 small tomato

2 medium red peppers

1 tbsp of ground chia seeds

salt

1 tbsp of olive oil

Preparation:

Wash and pat dry the vegetables using a kitchen paper. Cut into slices or strips. Heat up the olive oil over a medium temperature and fry the vegetables for about 10 minutes, stirring constantly. Add chia seeds and mix well. You want to wait until the vegetables soften and add eggs. Fry for another 2-3 minutes. Remove from the heat and serve.

Nutrition information per serving: Kcal: 190 Protein: 15.7g, Carbs: 2g, Fats: 14.6g

53. Chicken Wings

Ingredients:

12 to 18 chicken wings

1 teaspoon ground ginger

1 tablespoon honey

2 teaspoons olive oil

1/3 cup Worcestershire Sauce

2 minced green onions

2 minced garlic cloves

Preparation:

You simply have to apply all the ingredients on the chicken wings and put them in the pot. Set the heat to low-medium and cook for about an hour. The wings should be golden brown in color indicating they have been well-cooked. You can add spices according to your liking. Serve as an appetizer with ketchup or any sauce you like.

Nutrition information per serving: Kcal: 82 Protein: 7.8g, Carbs: 1.5g, Fats: 5.8g

54. Beans and spinach

Ingredients:

1 cup of canned green beans

1 cup of chopped spinach

2 cans of tuna, without oil

1 tbsp of olive oil

1 tsp of red wine vinegar

salt to taste

1 tbsp of ground turmeric

Preparation:

Combine the green beans with chopped spinach and tuna. Season with olive oil, vinegar, and salt. Add some turmeric before serving.

Nutrition information per serving: Kcal: 318 Protein: 12.3g, Carbs: 36.7g, Fats: 17.1g

55. Light turkey lunch

Ingredients:

3 thin slices of smoked turkey breast

1 cup of lettuce

1 small tomato

1 small onion

1 red pepper

1 tbsp of lemon juice

salt to taste

Preparation:

Cut the vegetables into small pieces. Combine them with turkey breast slices and season with salt and lemon juice.

Nutrition information per serving: Kcal: 190 Protein: 15.2g, Carbs: 18.3g, Fats: 6g

56. Tuna with olives

Ingredients:

2 cups of canned tuna without oil

1 cup of chopped lettuce

1 small onion

½ cup of olives

¼ cup of chopped red pepper

1 tbsp of olive oil

salt

1 tbsp of lemon juice

Preparation:

Peel and cut the onion into small pieces. Combine it with canned tuna and chopped lettuce. Mix well. Add olives and chopped red pepper. Season with olive oil, salt, and lemon juice. Keep in the refrigerator for about 20-30 minutes.

Nutrition information per serving: Kcal: 350 Protein: 20.2g, Carbs: 21.2g, Fats: 19.7g

57. Cottage cheese with lime dressing

Ingredients:

2 cups of cottage cheese

1 large cucumber

½ cup of ground walnuts

¼ cup of lime juice

¼ cup of low fat cream

1 tsp of lime extract

1 tbsp of olive oil

¼ tsp of pepper

Preparation:

First, you want to make a lime dressing. Mix the lime juice with low fat cream, lime extract, and olive oil. Add some pepper (this part depends on your taste). Mix well and leave in the fridge for about 30 minutes. Peel and cut the cucumber into small cubes and combine with ground walnuts and cottage cheese. Pour the dressing over your salad and serve cold.

Nutrition information per serving: Kcal: 201 Protein: 18.2g, Carbs: 26.4g, Fats: 1.5g

58. Creamy lentils

Ingredients:

1 cup of canned lentil

1 small eggplant

¼ cup of low fat cream

¼ cup of lemon juice

2 tbsp of olive oil

1 tbsp of chopped parsley

1 large tomato

1 small onion

Preparation:

Peel and wash the eggplant. Cut into thin slices and combine with a low fat cream, lemon juice, and olive oil. Use an electric mixer or a blender to get a smooth mousse. Allow it to cool in the refrigerator for about 30 minutes. Meanwhile cut the vegetables into thin slices. Mix with lentil and eggplant mousse. Sprinkle with some parsley and serve.

Nutrition information per serving: Kcal: 287 Protein: 17.2g, Carbs: 30.3g, Fats: 11.7g

ADDITIONAL TITLES FROM THIS AUTHOR

70 Effective Meal Recipes to Prevent and Solve Being Overweight: Burn Fat Fast by Using Proper Dieting and Smart Nutrition

By

Joe Correa CSN

48 Acne Solving Meal Recipes: The Fast and Natural Path to Fixing Your Acne Problems in Less Than 10 Days!

By

Joe Correa CSN

41 Alzheimer's Preventing Meal Recipes: Reduce or Eliminate Your Alzheimer's Condition in 30 Days or Less!

By

Joe Correa CSN

70 Effective Breast Cancer Meal Recipes: Prevent and Fight Breast Cancer with Smart Nutrition and Powerful Foods

By

Joe Correa CSN

www.ingramcontent.com/pod-product-compliance
Lightning Source LLC
Chambersburg PA
CBHW052020070526
44584CB00016B/1835